D1605419

An Illustrated Guide to
RUNES

An Illustrated Guide
to
RUNES

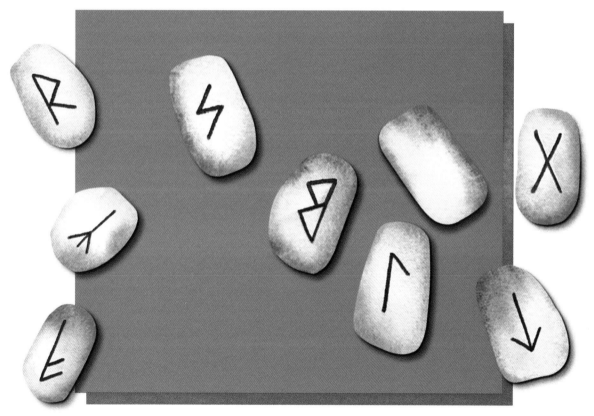

JONATHAN DEE

GRAMERCY

This 2001 edition is published by Gramercy Books™, an imprint of
Random House Value Publishing, Inc., 280 Park Avenue, New York,
NY 10017, by arrangement with D&S Books, Cottage Meadow, Bocombe,
Parkham, Bideford, Devon, England, EX39 5PH.

Gramercy Books™ and design are trademarks of Random House Value
Publishing, Inc.

Printed in Indonesia.

Random House
New York ● Toronto ● London ● Sydney ● Auckland
http://www.randomhouse.com/

A catalog record for this title is available from the
Library of Congress

ISBN: 0–517–16396–9

987654321

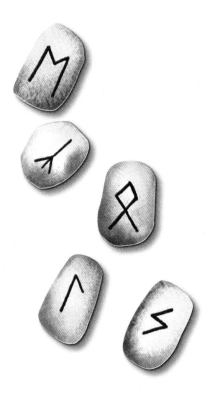

Contents

Introduction 6
The History of the Runes 9
The Gods of the North 12
The Vanir and the Aesir 14
The Sacrifice of Odin 17
The Norns 18
The Nine Worlds 19

The First Sequence – Frey's Aett 22
Fehu 25
Uruz 27
Thurisaz 30
Ansuz 33
Raido 36
Kaunaz 39
Gebo 42
Wunjo 45

The Second Sequence – Hagal's Aett 48
Hagalaz 50
Nauthiz 53
Isa 56
Jera 59
Eihwaz 62
Pertho 65
Algiz 68
Sowelo 71

The Third Sequence – Tyr's Aett 74
Tiwaz 76
Berkana 79
Ehwaz 82
Mannaz 85
Laguz 88
Inguz 91
Othila 94
Dagaz 97

Wyrd: the Blank Rune 100
The Art of Reading Runes 102
The Runic Calendar 118
Runic Initials 123

Index 126
Bibliography 128

Introduction

The runes were once the sacred alphabet of the Germanic peoples of Northern Europe. They were also used as a system of divination in a similar manner to the more modern Tarot cards. The very name "rune" derives from the ancient Gothic "runa," meaning a secret or a mystery. However, unlike the cards, the runes literally "spelled" words of power to be carved on amulets, rings, and weapons, and also as inscriptions on tombstones. In fact, the verb "spell" may come

The word "runa," from which "rune" is derived, literally means "secret." Likewise, the seventy-eight cards of the Tarot deck are divided into two parts called the major and minor arcana. The word "arcana" literally means "secret" or "mystery."

from ancient rune masters because it means "to make magic" and "to set out the letters of a words properly."

The most ancient complete runic alphabet comprises a series of twenty-four angular figures and is called the Elder Futhark. Just as the ancient Greek letters *alpha* and *beta* give us the word alphabet, the word "futhark" derives from the names of the first six runes. As time went on, the languages of certain Germanic peoples altered, causing an equivalent alteration in the written forms of their runic symbols. The Younger Futhark has only sixteen runes, while the Northumbrian Futhark used in Northern England began to include elements of Celtic culture and increased in size to thirty-three. Elsewhere, the runic tally was increased to thirty-

six. However, the Elder Futhark is the only rune-row directly to relate to the seasons of the year, the hours of the day, the directions of the compass, and other concepts of symbolic importance to our ancestors.

In today's world, the runes are usually drawn or carved onto a variety of small objects, such as slivers of wood or pebbles, or even molded into plastic "rune stones." There are many types of runes, or even rune cards available commercially. However, the rune masters of old would undoubtedly have recommended making your own set of runes by

An engraved rune stone from Mojbro, 7th century A.D., depicting a warrior on horseback followed by his dogs.

Runic Symbols and their Variations

MODERN LETTER OR SOUND	ELDER FUTHARK	YOUNGER FUTHARK	NORWEGIAN & ICELANDIC RUNES	GERMANIC RUNES
F	ᚠ	ᚡ	ᚡ	ᚡ
U	ᚢ	ᚢ	ᚢ	ᚢ
Th	ᚦ	ᚦ	ᚦ	ᚦ
A	ᚨ	ᚨ	ᚨ	ᚨ
R	ᚱ	ᚱ	ᚱ	ᚱ
K	ᚲ	ᚴ	ᚴ	ᚲ
G	ᚷ			ᚷ
W	ᚹ			ᚹ
H	ᚺ	ᚼ	ᚼ	ᚻ
N	ᚾ	ᚾ	ᚾ	ᚾ
I	ᛁ	ᛁ	ᛁ	ᛁ
J or Y	ᛃ	ᛄ	ᛄ	ᛃ
E	ᛂ			ᛂ
P	ᛈ			ᛈ
Z	ᛉ	ᛉ		ᛉ
S	ᛋ	ᛋ	ᛋ	ᛋ
T	ᛏ	ᛏ	ᛐ	ᛏ
B	ᛒ	ᛒ	ᛒ	ᛒ
E	ᛖ	ᛦ	ᛖ	ᛖ
M	ᛗ		ᛦ	ᛗ
L	ᛚ	ᛚ	ᛚ	ᛚ
NG	ᛜ	ᛢ		ᛥ
O	ᛟ			ᛟ
D	ᛞ	ᛞ		ᛞ

The 'New' Northumbrian Runes

MODERN LETTER OR SOUND	'NEW' RUNE	RUNE NAME	MEANING
short 'A'	ᛘ	Ac	Oak tree
AE	ᛟ	Aesc or Oss	Mouth, speech, song, language
Y	ᚣ	Yr	The yew bow, being on target
IO	ᛡ	Ior	Water beast
EA	ᛠ	Ear	Death, the grave, inevitable ending
Q	ᚳ	Cweorth	Cleansing by fire
K	ᚸ	Calc	Transformation
ST	ᛥ	Stan	Stone
G	ᚷ	Gar	Odin's spear

carving them with care into the wood of a fruit-bearing tree or painting them in red on small stones, or, failing that, by drawing them (again in red) on pieces of card.

Whatever your own personal runes happen to be made of, you should begin by familiarizing yourself with the simple shapes that make up the runic letters themselves. In this book, each of the runes is fully described, together with the symbolic images, such as the animals, trees, herbs, and celestial phenomena, associated with them. The myths of the Viking gods are also included to give a flavor of each of the individual runes. The more familiar you are with these stories, characteristics, and related concepts, the easier you will find it to read the runes properly and to use them as a sort of springboard for your own intuition.

The ancient art of casting the runes practiced by the rune masters of the Northern European peoples at the time of the Roman Empire can easily be mastered to this day. It is part of that tradition that the runes should be cast onto a plain white cloth to symbolize their purity.

It is important to remember that the runes are special and should be treated as such. Part of this specialness should be expressed in the way you keep your runes when they are not in use. Traditionally, runes should be kept in a drawstring bag to preserve them from hostile vibrations. It is also a good idea to keep a plain, white square of cloth in your runebag. This cloth should be placed on the table before you begin your reading to create a symbolic background to your rune-casting.

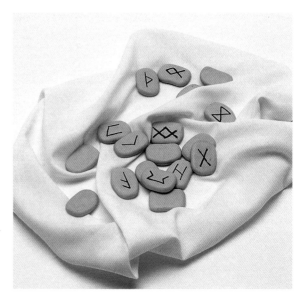

The History of the Runes

Even before the runes had achieved the status of a fully-fledged alphabet, the peoples of ancient Europe had carved their symbols into stones and trees to mark their territories and to represent their religious convictions. Symbols of this type are known as "Ur-runes" and are the ancestors of the runic forms we know today.

It is likely that the alphabetic order of the runes derives from the written language of the

The beautiful, but harsh, landscape of Iceland molded the thoughts of the Viking inhabitants of that distant land and caused them to adapt the Elder Futhark into their own version of the hallowed runic alphabet.

Etruscans, inhabitants of Northern Italy. The Germanic tribes in the Alps, modern-day Switzerland, and Austria combined the Etruscan forms of writing with their own traditional symbols and spread this knowledge among their kindred tribes.

From the very beginning, runes were thought to be magical in nature. They were used for the casting of lots to foretell the future and for magic to influence harvests and sea voyages, to curse, to bless, and to make love spells. They were also carved into sword blades to make them more deadly, into shields so that they would provide added protection, and into rings and necklaces to increase the beauty of their wearers.

True mastery of the runes was a highly respected skill

Runes on a gold ring.

of the wise men and women of those times. Those who had endured the ordeals of initiation into the mysteries of the runes were called rune masters and were considered separate from, and superior to, the general mass

ing at the end of the 1st century A.D., provided a description of the Teutonic peoples in his book *Germania*. Although Tacitus was mainly concerned with the customs, physique, and warlike nature of the tribes to the north of the

'She wore a cloak set with stones along the hem. Around her neck and covering her head she wore a hood lined with white cat-skins. In one hand she carried a staff with a knob on the end and from her belt, holding together her long dress, hung a charm pouch.'

'THE SAGA OF ERIK THE RED'

of the populace. In the Norse "Saga of Erik the Red," there is a description of a woman who was wise in the ways of the runes:

The ancient Roman historian Tacitus, writ-

Alps, he also provided the first-known account of runic divinations—see below.

It does not take much of an imagination to identify "the certain marks" as runic symbols

'No people practise augury and divination by lot more diligently. The use of the lots is simple. A little bough is lopped off a fruit-bearing tree, and cut into small pieces: these are distinguished by certain marks, and thrown carelessly at random over a white garment. In public the priest of the particular state, in private the father of the family, invokes the gods, and with his eyes towards heaven, takes up each piece three times, and finds in them a meaning according to the mark previously impressed upon them. If they prove unfavourable, there is no further consultation that day about the matter."

GERMANIA, BY TACITUS

cut into the wood of the "fruit-bearing tree." Tacitus also describes divinations taken from the flights of birds, the neighing of horses, and the course of battle between two combatants. Be that as it may, the practice of casting the runes is virtually identical to one of the methods employed today (see page 105).

After Christianity was introduced to Scandinavia and Iceland during the early medieval period, use of the runes for divination or in talismans was frowned upon as being akin to witchcraft. There are accounts, for example, of a man being burned at the stake simply for possessing a dice cup engraved with the rune Pertho, which was believed to aid gamblers. Nevertheless, the runic arts continued secretly in Iceland until the death of the last of the great rune masters in the middle of the 17th century, which ended an unbroken mystical tradition that was then over two thousand years old. However, this was not the end of the story for the runes. The 19th century saw a revival of interest, not only in the runes, but in the Nordic past in general. The mystical traditions of the Germanic peoples were again a focus for those who wished to renew their link with an almost mythical past. However, this also

had a dark side in the form of extreme nationalism and overt racism, especially in the works of Guido von List, who invented a "restored" version of the ancient Nordic alphabet that he called the "Armanen runes." Von List provided these runes complete with suitably twisted interpretations, the better to fit in with his own fascist ideology. It was the Armanen runes that were used by the Nazis in Germany as a source for their swastika symbol, along with S.S. insignia, and to further their sinister form of neopagan nationalism. It is this connection of the runes with Nazi symbolism that brought the runes into disrepute during the postwar period.

It was only at the end of the 20th century that the original purpose of the runes, now shorn of the dubious symbolism that had been thrust upon them, was restored. Today, the twenty-four runes of the Elder Futhark can be a helpful guide to the mysterious web of Wyrd that governs the fate of all of us.

A rune stone dating from the 11th century A.D. from Funbo, near Uppsala, dedicated by Tjagan and Gunnar to brother Vader.

A buckle clasp in silver, gold, and precious stones from Admark, Norway, 7th century A.D.

The Gods of the North

A picture stone with runic writing across the top. It has been suggested the standing figure in the house is Odin. (Viking, 11th century, Sweden.)

To gain a more complete understanding of the mysteries of the runes, it is necessary to digress a little into the myths and beliefs of the early Germanic peoples and, in particular, to find out about their gods and religious convictions.

In his book *Germania*, the ancient Roman author Tacitus wrote of the divinatory techniques of the ancient Germanic peoples and also attempted to describe their gods. He states that Mercury is the chief of their deities, but also that Hercules, Isis, and Mars are worshiped. In

describing the gods by names familiar to the Romans, Tacitus reveals something of the nature of these divinities. In this case, Mercury, the cunning, swift-witted Roman god of commerce, travel, and divination, can easily be identified with Odin or Wotan. Hercules, with his mighty club, can be seen as the equally formidable hammer-wielding Thor, while Isis, Queen of Heaven, is probably the cloud-weaving Frigga. Likewise, Mars, god of war, can be read as Tyr or Tiwaz (see Tiwaz, page 76). The Roman author reinforces the point by stating that the Teutonic peoples are descended from an earth-born god called Tuisco (Tiwaz) and his son Mannus (Mannaz, page 85). Tacitus therefore gives us more information about Germanic religion and the basis of the Germanic people's belief in the runes than even he can possibly have suspected.

To learn more about these mysterious divinities and, indeed, other gods worshiped by the Germanic and Norse peoples, we have to turn to the epic tales, poems, and sagas of Iceland. These were written in the medieval period and reflect a time of wild pagan adventurers some centuries in the writers' past. In these tales, the myths and characters of the Norse gods have been preserved.

Figurine, probably a chessman, which may represent Thor (Viking, Denmark.)

A family tree of the Norse gods, with their associated runes

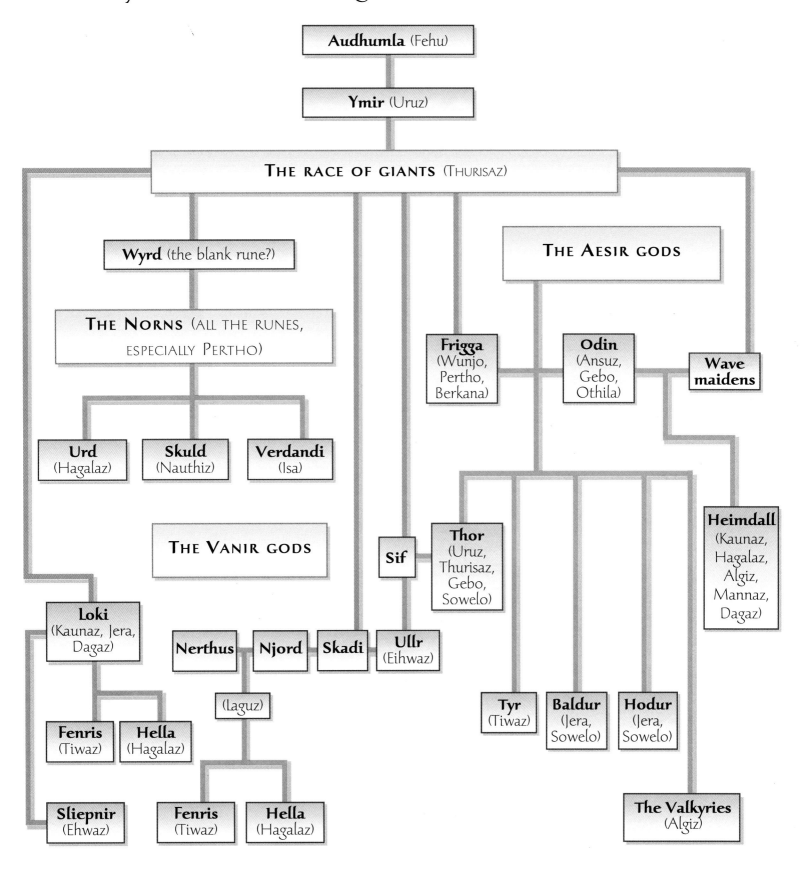

The Vanir and the Aesir

Frey, god of fertility. Front view. (Viking, 11th century, Sweden.)

It is important to note that there is more than one type of god in the northern pantheon. Apart from the chaotic giants of frost and fire who were said to dwell on the fringes of creation, the divinities of order were divided into two main families: the Aesir and the Vanir. The Vanir seem to have predated the other gods, being pastoral deities associated with harvests, the fertility of beasts and humans, and, not least, the earth itself. The most notable of the Vanir were the children of Njord (see Laguz, page 88), the beloved twins Frey and Freya, whose names mean "the lord" and "the lady" respectively (see Fehu, page 25; Raido, page 36; Ehwaz, page 82; Algiz, page 68; and Inguz, page 91).

The other godly dynasty was known as the Aesir. These were headed by Odin and his wife, Frigga, and it is among these deities that we find such familiar characters as Thor, the thunder god, and Tyr, god of war, both sons of Odin. Of course, as king of the gods, Odin was expected to have many sons, and among them can be numbered Baldur the Beautiful and his twin brother, Hodur the Blind, representing light and dark, day and night, and summer and winter (see Jera, page 59, and Dagaz, page 97). The guardian of Asgard and the rainbow bridge that led to it was the ever-watchful Heimdall, himself a result of the union of Odin with nine sea giantesses, known as the wave maidens (though we shall swiftly pass over the problem of how Heimdall managed to have nine mothers). Heimdall was the god "who stood between," the ancestor of humankind who revealed the secrets of the runes to his mortal descendants. As might be expected, he figures largely in runic symbolism, having associations with no fewer than five runes out of the twenty-four in the rune sequence (see Kaunaz, page 39; Hagalaz, page 50; Algiz, page 68; Mannaz, page 85; and Dagaz, page 97).

Detail of a forge stone incised with the face of the god Loki with his lips sewn together. (late Viking period, Denmark.)

Before we leave the realm of Asgard, there is one god who is something of an anomaly: the treacherous Loki, born of the race of giants and the hated rival of Heimdall. Loki personifies wild, uncontrollable fire, in contrast to his enemy, Heimdall, who symbolizes a torch or beacon, a friend to humankind. Nevertheless, Loki was blood brother to Odin, and his mischief was tolerated because of that kinship. However, Loki must have stretched the divine patience considerably, because it was he who caused the death of Baldur (see Jera, page 59), and even though Sleipnir, one of his children, was considered benign (see Ehwaz, page 82), it was also he who was parent to the vile Hella (see Hagalaz, page 50) and the monstrous wolf, Fenris (see Tiwaz, page 76), who tried to destroy the universe and was fated to devour Odin at the end of the world at Ragnarok, the "Twilight of the Gods."

Wood panel depicting Odin being swallowed by Fenris. (Iceland.)

The Gods of the Runes

DEITY OR SYMBOLIC BEING(S)	FUNCTION	ASSOCIATED RUNE(S)		BASIC MEANING
Audhumla the Cow	Primordial Being	ᚠ	Fehu	Prosperity
The Auroch Bull	Masculine Power	ᚢ	Uruz	Ferocity
Thor	Thunder God	ᚦ	Thurisaz	Boundaries
Odin	Supreme God	ᚨ	Ansuz	Trials and Divine inspirations
Frery/Ing	Fertility/Horse God	ᚱ	Raido	Honour
Heimdall	The Sentinel	ᚲ	Kaunaz	Knowledge
Odin & Thor	Gift Givers	ᚷ	Gebo	Generosity
Frigga	The Virtuous Wife	ᚹ	Wunjo	Happy Endings
Urd (also Hella)	The Norn of the Past	ᚺ	Hagalaz	Hail and Sleet
Verdandi	The Norn of the Future	ᚾ	Nauthiz	Necessity
Skuld (also Rind)	The Norn of the Present	ᛁ	Isa	Ice, Cold, Iron
Baldur & Hudur (also cunning Loki)	Gods of Light and Dark	ᛃ	Jera	Joy, Celebration
Ullr	God of Hunting	ᛇ	Eihwaz	Adaptibility
The Three Norns and also Frigga	Weavers of the Web of Fate	ᛈ	Pertho	Chance and Destiny
The Valkyries and also Heimdall	Choosers of the Slain	ᛉ	Algiz	Healing and Protection
Baldur and also Thor	Gods of Light and Justice	ᛊ	Sowelo	Life Force, Love and Poetic Justice
Tyr	One handed God of War and Oaths	ᛏ	Tiwaz	Binding Agreements
Frigga in her form as Brechta	Mother Goddess	ᛒ	Berkano	Birth, Living Things epecially vegetation
Frey/Ing and also Sliepnir	Fertility/Horse God	ᛖ	Ehwaz	Adventure and also the animal kingdom
Heimdall in his form as Rigr	The God who Stands Between	ᛗ	Mannaz	Mankind
Njord and Nerthus	Gods of Safe Harbours	ᛚ	Laguz	Spiritual Love
Frey/Ing	God of Fertility	ᛜ	Inguz	Health, Fertility
Odin	King of the Gods, The All–father"	ᛟ	Othila	Rulership and Nobility, Loyalty, Inheritance
Heimdall and Loki	Rival Gods of Order and Chaos respectively	ᛞ	Dagaz	Midsummer, beginnings and endings, breakthrough

The sacrifice of Odin

The two families of gods once fought a war in which the Vanir were the victors due to their ability to predict the future. This was a gift that Odin was determined to gain for himself. After peace was declared, hostages were exchanged as a guarantee against future hostilities. Odin's brother, Hoenir, went to live in Vanaheim, home of the Vanir, while Njord and his children, Frey and Freya, made their abode in Odin's realm of Asgard. Once this exchange was accomplished, Odin decided to put himself through a terrible ordeal, and for nine days and nights hung from the world tree, Yggdrasil, wounded by his own spear:

'Wounded I hung on a wind-swept gallows
For nine long nights, pierced by a spear,
Pledged to Odin, offered myself to myself.
The wisest know not from whence spring
The roots of that ancient tree.

They gave me no bread,
They gave me no mead,
I looked down;
With a loud cry I took up runes;
From that tree I fell.'

THE HAVAMAL' OR THE 'SONG OF ODIN'

By this self-sacrifice, Odin gained the knowledge of the runes. However, he still did not think that he had sufficient wisdom to use them, so in order that he might drink from the well of memory, Odin paid a terrible price by plucking out one of his own eyes.

Now Odin had knowledge of the future, yet he still did not believe that he knew enough, so he turned to the Vanir goddess Freya and persuaded her to teach him magic. Only then did Odin finally feel that his position as king of the gods was secure . . . at least, until Ragnarok, the day of doom that had been fated by the web of Wyrd. For although Odin had the knowledge of the runes, it was the implacable Norns who first wrote them.

Tapestry detail. On the left, one-eyed Odin is carrying an axe, with a representation of the tree from which he hung. Thor is in the center, and Frey on the right. (Viking, 12th century, Sweden.)

The Norns

'Thence come three maidens who much do know;

Three from the hall beneath the tree;

*One they named **Was**, the second **Is**,*

*These two fashioned a third, named **Shall Be**.*

They established law,

They selected lives

For the children of time,

And the fates of men.'

'THE VOLUSPA'

The three sisters who were the Norns, or goddesses of fate, were not part of either of the divine families (although they do seem to have had some affinity with the Vanir). They formed a separate group and were considered to be subject to nothing save the dictates of necessity (occasionally personified as their mother, Wyrd). These goddesses represent time itself and were therefore thought of as women of differing ages. Urd, the Norn of the past, was thought of as being very old and decrepit, always looking backward to the way things were. The young and vibrant Verdandi, Norn of the present, looked fearlessly ahead, while Skuld, the mysterious Norn of the future, was depicted as veiled, holding a scroll that had not yet been opened. Two of the Norns, Urd and Verdandi, were said to be more kindly than their sister Skuld, who often undid their work, angrily scattering the almost finished patterns before they had come to fruition.

The Norns dwelled at the roots of the great world tree, Yggdrasil, and it was part of their job to sprinkle it with water drawn from the well of fate to ensure that it developed as destiny demanded. Principally, though, the Norns wove the web of Wyrd that set out the fates of gods and humans. Legend has it that they wove designs so awesome in scope that if one of them stood on a mountaintop in the farthest east and another waded far into the ocean in the farthest west, the full extent of their pattern could still never be fully seen.

The concept of three prophetic witches survived the pagan period in Europe and entered folklore both as the three good fairies who bestowed gifts on Sleeping Beauty and, in a more sinister guise, as the three "Weird sisters" of Shakespeare's play *Macbeth*.

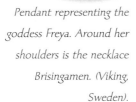

Pendant representing the goddess Freya. Around her shoulders is the necklace Brisingamen. (Viking, Sweden).

A carving on the side of the stave church at Urnes depicts the deer eating the world tree, Yggdrasil. (Viking, Norway.)

The Nine Worlds

Norse mythology also speaks of nine worlds that make up the created universe. These worlds are all connected by the roots and branches of the great world tree, Yggdrasil, as well as being subject to the web of Wyrd. Odin, as the prototype shaman-priest, traveled freely through these worlds on the back of his mighty eight-legged stallion, Sleipnir. Likewise, the sorcerers of the northern tribes would go on dream journeys in search of enlightenment, using the runic symbols as talismans and keys to other realms of existence.

Detail of a carved funerary stone. The top panel depicts Odin mounted on his eight-legged steed, Sleipnir. (Viking, 8th century, Sweden.)

The first of the nine worlds is our own, called by the Vikings, as well as those who came before them, Midgard. This means "Middle Earth," the world of mortal humans. Students of the history and traditions of the Norse people have been confused by the fact that the later Vikings also described the city of Constantinople as Midgard, probably in the belief that this great metropolis was the very center of the Middle Earth.

To the north of Midgard lay Nifelheim, or Nifelhel, the world of the serpent Nidhog, the "gnawer from beneath." This was the realm of ice and cold, and located here was one of the three wells that nourished the roots of the world tree. However, Nidhog continually chewed this root to cause the earth to freeze in eternal snows.

Jotunheim, or the "giant world," lay on the fringes of creation. It was the home of the vast primal powers, personified as giants who wished to bring chaos and ruin to the universe. However, many of the giantesses were more kindly disposed than their menfolk. Even so, the might of the hammer of Thor was

The awesome and uncontrollable powers of nature were personified as the monstrous race of giants who dwelt on Jotunheim, at the very fringes of creation. However, nature also has a kindly face, which is why the Vikings thought that many of the giantesses were much nicer than their menfolk.

The rainbow bridge connected Midgard (Middle Earth), where humans lived to Asgard, the realm of the gods.

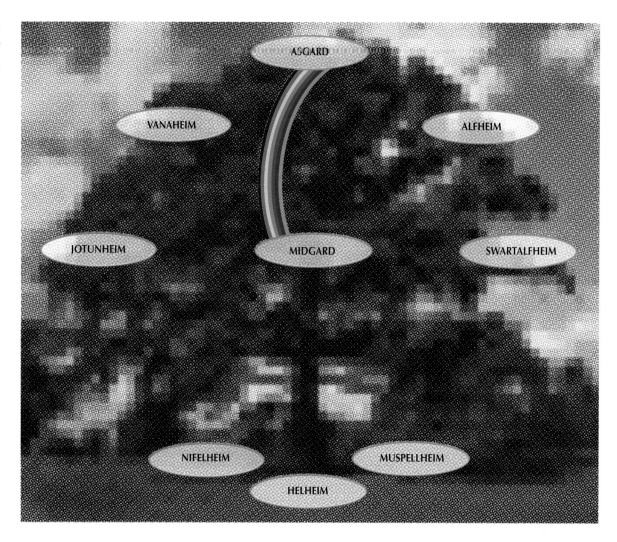

The greatest safeguard against the ill will of these titans. Jotunheim was also the location of the well of memory that nourished another of the roots of Yggdrasil.

To the south of Midgard was Muspellheim, the world of fire. Here, equally fearsome giants made their abode. These monsters were led by Surtr, who desired to bathe the universe in flame. Again, the might of Thor was necessary to hold the fire giants at bay.

In total contrast to these violent realms, Vanaheim, original home of the Vanir gods, was a gentle world of calm seas, fertile lands, and abundance.

After Vanaheim was Alfheim, the world of the elves. These elves should not be thought of as the small, gossamer-winged creatures of Victorian sentiment, but as powerful, mysterious and wonderful beings who were the souls of nature. Their king was Frey, god of fertility.

Swartalfheim, or the world of the dark elves, better known as dwarves or gnomes, came next. This world was thought to be sub-terranean because it was believed that this sort of supernatural creature could not stand the light of day. The dwarves made marvelous weapons, jewelry, and other artifacts for the gods.

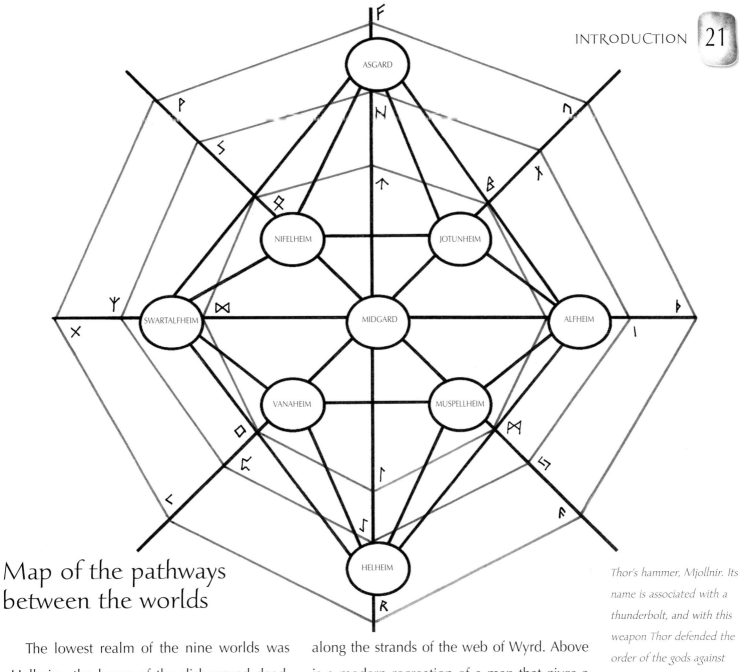

Map of the pathways between the worlds

The lowest realm of the nine worlds was Helheim, the home of the dishonored dead. A shadowy kingdom of broken dreams and long regrets, the queen of this dolorous realm was Hella, the daughter of Loki.

The highest world was Asgard, home of the Aesir gods and the location of Valhalla, the home of Odin and the honored dead, as well as the palaces of the other gods. Access to this world was via the rainbow bridge eternally guarded by Heimdall.

The runic masters of old believed that there were magical pathways between these worlds along the strands of the web of Wyrd. Above is a modern recreation of a map that gives a close approximation of the routes that these mystic dream travelers took. Those who are familiar with the tree of life in cabalistic tradition will detect many similarities between the two belief systems. You may also notice that each junction of the pathways or strands is governed by a rune. The outer strands relate to the first aett, the second set of stands to the second aett, and so it goes on.

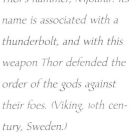

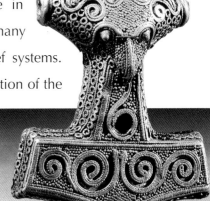

Thor's hammer, Mjollnir. Its name is associated with a thunderbolt, and with this weapon Thor defended the order of the gods against their foes. (Viking, 10th century, Sweden.)

THE FIRST SEQUENCE: Frey's Aett

The runes of the Elder Futhark are divided into three groups, each comprising eight runes in a specific order. The first of these is called Frey's Aett, after the beloved god of fertility and beginnings. It is from this aett that the word "futhark" comes. The first six runes spell this out in the same way that the Greek *alpha* and *beta* give us the word "alphabet." The order of the rune-row in Frey's Aett is as follows: Fehu, Uruz, Thurisaz, Ansuz, Raido, Kaunaz, Gebo, and, finally, Wunjo. Frey's Aett is said to contain the secrets of creation and the order in which events

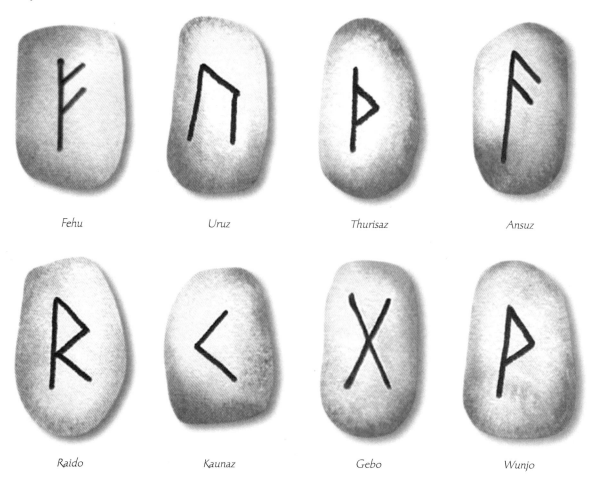

Fehu   *Uruz*   *Thurisaz*   *Ansuz*

Raido   *Kaunaz*   *Gebo*   *Wunjo*

occurred at the very beginning of time. Out of the opposing forces of fire and ice was born the primordial being, Audhumla, symbolized by the cow shown in the first rune, Fehu. The wild bull, Uruz, follows. The next being, the giant Ymir, is symbolized by the next rune, Thurisaz, meaning "giant." Then the gods came into being, as shown by Ansuz, a rune that means "god." The gods set the cycle of life in motion, symbolized by a wheel, hence the rune Raido. This cycle is also represented as time and the division between day and night, and so we come to the next rune in the sequence, Kaunaz, which is a torch or a bonfire. This is a symbolic representation of the Sun by day and the Moon at night. Now the gods, led by Odin, created humankind by giving the gift of life to two trees, the ash and the elm. The rune Gebo symbolizes that gift, and also the dutiful gratitude owed by mortals to the gods who created them. With Wunjo, we reach the rune of perfection, because everything is now in its place and the universe, as imagined by the ancient Northern European peoples, is complete.

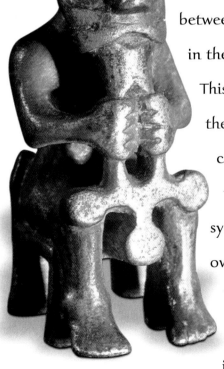

Thor, god of thunder. (Viking, c. 1000 A.D., Iceland.)

A relief sculpture of Scandinavian origin from the Gosforth Churchyard, believed to depict Thor fishing with the giant Ymir. (Viking, England.)

Fehu

"THE FIRST CHARM I KNOW IS UNKNOWN TO KINGS OR ANY OF MAN-KIND.

Help is it named for help it can give in hours of sorrow and anguish."

"THE HAVAMAL" OR "SONG OF ODIN"

ALTERNATIVE NAMES

In the Anglo-Saxon system, this rune is known as Feoh, while the Vikings knew it as Fe.

PRONUNCIATION

"F."

KEY CONCEPTS

This is the first rune of the first aett, so it is associated with beginnings, but, even more importantly, with property, reputation, status, and wealth, which the ancient northern cultures measured by the possession of abundant herds of cattle. This rune is considered to be feminine and maternal in nature.

Because cattle were synonymous with wealth to the people of the ancient world, the rune Fehu, which represents a cow, also symbolizes financial well-being, security, and prosperity.

The ancient Vikings believed that the first being, the great cow Audhumla, licked away a vast block of ice to free the ancestral giant Ymir.

MYTHOLOGY

According to the sagas of Iceland, which, although composed during the Middle Ages, recorded the beliefs of the ancient Norse, the first living creature was a cow called Audhumla. This cosmic animal was born from the union of fire and ice that predated the creation of the nine worlds. Coming into existence in an environment barren of nourishment, Audhumla licked a great block of ice, thus freeing the giant Ymir, who either lay within it or was shaped by the actions of the great cow's tongue. Ymir became the ancestor of the gods, humans, and the later race of giants, all of whom existed because of Audhumla and who continued to be nurtured by her, as are calves by their mothers.

The belief in Audhumla as the precursor of all that lives harks back to a remote time when the mother goddess was usually personified as a totem animal. In Greece, for example, Athena was imagined as an owl, while Aphrodite was envisaged a dove. In Nordic culture, the mother goddess is the gentle, milk-producing cow.

The rune Fehu is also directly related to some of Audhumla's Vanir descendants (see page 14), especially Njord and his children, the peace-loving Frey and the amorous Freya, each of whom have an association with wealth and fertility.

UPRIGHT MEANING

Fehu is obviously an indicator of prosperity. Before the introduction of hard currency, cattle herds were the measure of wealth among many ancient peoples. So when this rune is found in a future position, a profitable time lies before you. However, just as the ancients sacrificed one of their herd now and again to show the gods that they were thankful for their good fortune, it is equally important that you receive the gifts of Fehu with humility. The rune also suggests that you should look after the possessions that are already in your keeping and that you should guard your resources against times when the warmth of the comforting fire is chilled by the icy blast of winter. Even if you are comfortably off, you have an opportunity to ensure that this happy state continues. Conversely, if you are feeling

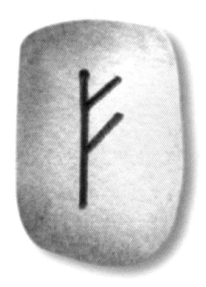

the bite of poverty, Fehu promises that the time will soon come when you will be prosperous once more. Aside from these material concerns, the appearance of Fehu bodes well for fertility, childbirth, and new beginnings of all kinds. Equally, as the "Song of Odin" states, when one is in misery or grief, the rune Fehu will bring motherly comfort, which is one of the most valuable things in the world.

INVERTED MEANING

A reversal of fortune resulting in the loss of something valuable is likely when this rune is inverted. The association of Fehu with wealth and property suggests that this loss will involve a material possession, but it may equally relate to the departure of a loved one or close friend. However, since the basic nature of Fehu is nurturing, the loss will be made up in time. Tradition also states that Fehu inverted may refer to problems with conception or fertility in general.

Uruz

"Ur is a wild and fierce beast possessing great horns. A formidable ranger of moorland, it fights with its horns. It is a beast of courage."

"THE ANGLO-SAXON RUNE POEM"

ALTERNATIVE NAMES

The Anglo-Saxons and Vikings both called this rune Ur.

PRONUNCIATION:

"U" or "OO."

KEY CONCEPTS

The name of the rune is primarily connected with the long-extinct wild bulls of the north, the aurochs. These untameable beasts roamed the wastelands and were much feared. However, the sound of the alternative name, Ur, creates a pun, both on the old Norse word for ore, hence metal, and on a word meaning hail or drizzle, hence inclement weather. As well as these subsidiary concepts, the syllable Ur can also be taken to mean "ancient" or "primordial." This is a fitting description for an animal of prehistoric power, such an auroch. This rune is considered masculine and forceful in nature.

The name "Uruz" has many levels of meaning, one of the most central being bad weather, hail and drizzle. This concept leads on to the idea of determination to withstand such difficulties.

The association of the rune with metal results in the symbolism of great strength that should be harnessed to good purpose. The chain pictured here represents the self-restraint necessary to use this mighty force wisely.

MYTHOLOGY

It is likely that Uruz originally represented the second half of a primordial pair, the first being the cow, Audhumla, symbolized by the first rune, Fehu. Uruz is undoubtedly masculine in character, and, indeed, there may have once been a mythological equivalent of the primitive mother goddess that was represented as a mighty bull god. If this was the case, then conformation of the theory has been lost over time. However, it is true that the most macho of the Viking gods was associated with this rune. Thor, the thunder god, the strong champion of the deities of Asgard and sworn enemy of the chaotic giants, was the divinity to whom the peoples of the north ascribed the rune Uruz. The subsidiary meanings of both hail and ore add credence to this attribution, since Thor was the god of the storm and wielder of a deadly hammer that was made for him by subterranean dwarves.

UPRIGHT MEANING

Powerful energies are at work when the rune Uruz appears. If you require added vitality, then Uruz is a good omen. However, you must treat this power with respect and caution, or its wild nature may cause you to regret the fact that you chose to use its force in the first place. After all, it is fairly easy to goad a bull into charging, but it is not as simple a matter to stop it when its job is done. This rune's association with courage and great strength means that it is certain that you will overcome any obstacles. However brute force will not be enough to see any changes through: you will also have to use your intelligence to harness the power of Uruz wisely.

This rune is considered good for healing, giving strength to those who have been ill and hastening recovery. Uruz may also indicate a rise in status, but first make sure that you are not biting off more than you can chew.

INVERTED MEANING

Weakness and physical or mental fatigue are indicated when Uruz is inverted. There may even be an underlying health problem, so perhaps it is time for a checkup or a thorough review of your lifestyle. There is a sense of being overwhelmed by events and not having the will to face up to reality when the rune appears in this position, so take care: powerful forces may be ranged against you.

Thurisaz

"The Thorn is most sharp, an evil thing to take a grip on, extremely grim for any man who rests among them."

"THE ANGLO-SAXON RUNE POEM"

ALTERNATIVE NAMES

To the Anglo-Saxons, this rune was Thorn, while to the Vikings it was known as Thurs.

PRONUNCIATION

"TH."

KEY CONCEPTS

The Thurisaz rune represents a sharp thorn. By extension of the idea, it also suggests a blade, knife, or a fang. Therefore the rune is also associated with the deadly bites of serpents. The sound of the letter, too, resembles the hiss of a snake, as well as the sound that a sword makes when it is drawn from a scabbard.

The rune Thurisaz is associated with sharp objects like thorns, knives, or the fangs of serpents. The rune therefore also symbolizes a deadly bite, while the sound that it makes is reminiscent of the hiss of a snake.

MYTHOLOGY

The first syllable of the rune, Thur, or Thurs, survives today in Thursday, the name of the fifth day of the week, which literally means "giant's day," but it is also associated with the mighty god Thor, who was something of a giant, even among the larger-than-life deities of Asgard. The rune's name, Thurisaz, was an ancient title of the thunder god, and it has been suggested by some that the form of the rune represents Thor's hammer, although others think that it merely shows a single thorn on a stem.

The Thurisaz rune represents a sharp thorn and therefore became associated with other sharp objects, such as blades. The sound that Thurisaz makes resembles a sword being drawn from its scabbard.

UPRIGHT MEANING

The rune Thurisaz suggests boundaries, which in old Norse times were often marked out by thickets of hawthorn. So by extension it is important to know your own limits when this rune appears. Hasty decisions made now will be regretted later, so it is definitely not a time to forge ahead regardless. Because of the rune's association with sharp objects, fangs, and snakes, Thurisaz may indicate a time of personal risk. There may be people around you who are being less than honest or who do not have your best interests at heart. In business matters especially, extreme care must be taken, for there is a danger of being let down or betrayed. However, this can only occur if you are not sufficiently vigilant, so be warned. The rune may show that you will soon have to

defend yourself and your actions in some way. However, it may also indicate that luck will arrive in the guise of a challenge. Tradition states that if used as a charm, this rune will blunt the words and weapons of your enemies.

INVERTED MEANING

If you are in any doubt about your actions, do nothing at all. If you act hastily now, you will have plenty of time in the future to repent your folly. An inverted Thurisaz emphasizes the warnings of its upright meaning and indicates that you are in danger of walking straight into a trap. It also shows that you are likely to play into the hands of your enemies and that your own rash actions will prove to be your undoing. Take a step back and review your situation. Pause, reflect, and then proceed very cautiously indeed.

Ansuz

"I know a fourth, it will free me quickly if foes should bind me fast with strong chains, a chant that makes fetters fall from the feet and bonds burst from the hands."

THE "SONG OF ODIN"

ALTERNATIVE NAMES

The Anglo-Saxons called this rune Os, while the Norsemen of Norway and Iceland referred to it as Oss.

PRONUNCIATION

"A" or "O" interchangeably, hence "futhark" may also be spelled "futhork."

KEY CONCEPTS

The fourth rune, Ansuz, is connected with the faculty of speech and, indeed, with the mouth itself. The variant word, Oss, was used both in connection with the organs of speech and in the sense of a river mouth. Apart from this, Oss also referred to the wise Odin, the one-eyed king of the gods of Asgard and ruler of Valhalla. For this reason, Ansuz is called the "god rune."

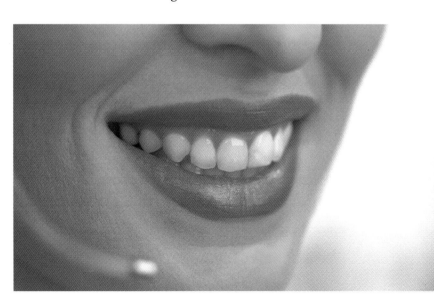

The faculty of speech sets humankind apart from animals and, to the rune masters of old, was proof of humans' essential divinity because it was an ability that they shared with the gods. The rune Ansuz represents both the human mouth and a river mouth, as well as being symbolic of cosmic forces.

It was said that Odin kept two ravens called Hugin and Munin, or "Thought" and "Memory," as pets. These carrion birds kept the god informed about everything that happened in the nine worlds.

MYTHOLOGY

Odin was considered to be the creator of the runes themselves, and Ansuz shares his attributes. Since Odin's companions were two ravens, Hugin and Munin, or "Thought" and "Memory," these carrion birds are associated with Ansuz, as well as the two fierce wolves that were also his pets. It is said that Odin hung for nine nights from the windy ash tree, Yggdrasil, to learn the secrets of the runes, and so the wood of the ash is connected with Ansuz. This sacrifice of Odin was repeated many times by those who wished to become proficient in rune magic. For this purpose, potential rune masters would put themselves through grueling physical ordeals to learn wisdom in the same terrible manner as their god. Hallucinogenic substances were also part of these trials, hence Ansuz is connected with the properties of the fly agaric toadstool.

UPRIGHT MEANING

Fast-changing situations are to be expected when the rune Ansuz is drawn. You may find yourself in a set of new circumstances with few clues about the correct way in which to proceed. However, even though the conscious mind may be at a loss, the unconscious knows better and will use dreams and strange coincidences to communicate guidance. The rune may also suggest that the influence of a helpful advisor will become a prominent feature in your life very soon. This person is likely to be male, with a great deal of worldly experience, and is probably of an older generation. The spoken word and the powers of persuasion are the basic meanings of this rune. It should be remembered that the runes are in themselves "words of power" that, as the "Song of Odin" states, can make "fetters fall from the feet and

bonds burst from the hands." Thus the appearance of Ansuz ensures that you can use your wits and verbal dexterity to remove yourself from restraints if you know, or can learn, the correct way to go about it. The god-rune aspect of Ansuz should not be ignored: a religious influence may be felt in some way, or you could feel touched by cosmic forces.

INVERTED MEANING

A loss of voice is shown by the inverted rune. This may be literally so – a case of laryngitis, perhaps – or, in a more symbolic sense, you will not be able to make yourself heard. Problems with communication in general are highlighted. Letters and documents may go astray and you could find yourself somewhat isolated for a while. There could also be hitches when traveling, or your thoughts could become confused. Problems with parents, or with older people in general, are also likely.

Raido

"Riding is easy for the warrior indoors, and very courageous to him who travels the high road upon a stout horse."

"THE ANGLO-SAXON RUNE POEM"

ALTERNATIVE NAMES

To the Anglo-Saxons, this rune was known as Rad; in Iceland, it was Reid; while to the Norwegian Vikings, it was known as Raid (aptly enough, for a piratical race), which actually means "riding."

PRONUNCIATION

"R."

KEY CONCEPTS

Raido is the rune of the Sun, pictured in the Norse imagination as a mighty cartwheel rolling across the sky. Thus the rune became connected with carts, land transportation in general, horses, and other pack animals. Because of the correspondence with the horse, Raido became the rune of those who rode: the nobility and rulers. Thus it not only meant "to ride," but gained the meaning of doing the right thing, acting honorably, and telling right from wrong. By association, Raido also gained an association with the oak tree, with the goats who pulled the chariot of Thor, and with the healing herb mugwort.

Raido is symbolically connected with the Sun, which the Germanic peoples pictured as a mighty cartwheel that revolved around the sky daily.

The rune Raido means "riding," and it is in connection with horses that its most potent symbolism is found. Sleipnir, the steed of Odin, as well as an obscure fertility god named Ing, who was depicted as a stallion, are its associated deities.

MYTHOLOGY

The most obvious mythological connection with the rune Raido is Odin's famous horse, Sleipnir, a fabulous steed with eight legs which could carry his master to all of the nine worlds of creation. However, tradition states that the rune is intimately connected with an obscure Teutonic fertility god called Ing, who may well have been imagined as a powerful stallion. Ing was a god of great importance to the early Anglo-Saxons. When they first came to the shores of Britain during the 5th and 6th centuries A.D., they bore the banner of the white stallion, which remains the emblem of the county of Kent, in Southern England, to this day. It is likely that Ing would have been completely forgotten by now were it not for the fact that the country of England owes its very name to him.

UPRIGHT MEANING

Journeys of all kinds, both in the outer world and in the personal, inner realm, are pictured when the rune Raido appears. The use of judgement, too, is indicated, with the advised course being to act honorably. Doing the right thing at all times will bring you the respect and admiration of those who matter. It also suggests that the road that you travel along may not always be easy, but that the eventual rewards will be worthl the trials and tribulations encountered along the way. Raido can be interpreted as a move forward in some venture, too. Legal and official affairs of all kinds will be resolved to your satisfaction and promises, oaths, and testimony will work to your benefit. However, this is not a rune about advice: in fact, the opposite is the case, since

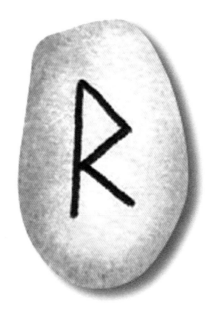

Raido clearly states that it is your own judgement that will outweigh any other point of view. Its appearance warns against confiding your plans to anyone, so keep your counsel, think deeply and once your mind is made up, do not waver from your course.

INVERTED MEANING

Disruptions of your plans are inevitable, but that does not mean that you can abandon your long-term intentions. The road you are traveling on may be rocky at the moment, but you should not be disheartened. Short-term problems may be pressing, but it is important that you do not lose sight of the bigger picture. A financial venture or legal dispute may not go the way you want, or you may purchase something that promises to solve one problem, but only creates more. Keep the faith: this troublesome period will not last forever.

Kaunaz

"Cen is known to all by its pale bright flame, it always burns where princes sit within."

"THE ANGLO-SAXON RUNE POEM"

ALTERNATIVE NAMES

The Anglo-Saxons called this rune Ken or Cen, while the ancient Norse referred to it as Kaun.

PRONUNCIATION

"K" or hard "C."

KEY CONCEPTS

Kaunaz is the flame of a torch cut from the branch of a pine tree. Its wan light keeps the darkness at bay and allows the sentinel to protect his charges from harm. The torch has other associations, too: it can symbolize learning, and especially the knowledge handed on from generation to generation, which is why the words Kaunaz and Ken are related to our words "kin" or "kindred." The symbolism of the flame can additionally be applied to passion, without which further generations would not exist. On the other hand, the word Kaun also resembles the Norse word for "wasting" or "ulcer," possibly because, when maintaining a flame, the kindling that provides its fuel is eventually consumed.

Kaunaz represents the bright flame of a torch or beacon fire that keeps darkness at bay and allows a watchman to keep his charges from harm.

The ever-vigilant owl is one of the symbolic creatures associated with Heimdall, the sentinel of the gods and the main deity of the rune Kaunaz.

MYTHOLOGY

The rune Kaunaz is associated with the trustworthy gatekeeper of the gods, Heimdall, a deity as mysterious and brooding as a pine forest. Heimdall was a son of Odin, and it was his job to prevent mortals and giants from crossing the rainbow bridge, Bifrost, as it was prophesied that they would do, thereby bringing about Ragnarok, or the "Twilight of the Gods." He was ever-watchful, and was thus identified with the vigilant owl. Heimdall was known as the "shining god," and was personified as a torch or beacon. He stood between Asgard and the world of humankind and is credited with passing on the knowledge of the runes to mortals. Bonfires and beacons lit on mountaintops in order to pass on news of great importance were likewise associated with Heimdall and his rune, Kaunaz.

UPRIGHT MEANING

The most obvious meaning of this rune is the gaining and passing on of knowledge. However, we should not forget its connection with passion, which can be felt in both a physical and a mental sense. One may be passionate about a subject or a person, for example, and when this rune appears in a reading, the two concepts are often strangely mixed together, just as the ancient Anglo-Saxon verb "kennen" meant both "to conceive" and "to bring forth from the mind." In more mundane terms, Kaunaz can mean the start of a consuming love affair and the spark of a meaningful relationship that may teach both parties a thing or two about life. This is one of the most positive runes, leading you on a path of new discovery. It is also an indicator of safety, because in some mystical sense you are being watched over as thoroughly as if Heimdall or the vigilant owl were guarding you from danger. A sudden, powerful insight is also likely when Kaunaz is prominent, and you may feel touched by a clarity of vision that you have never known before.

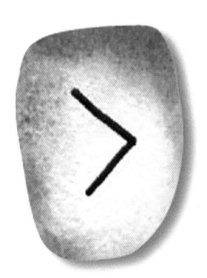

INVERTED MEANING

A loss of love, friendship, and old loyalties are foretold when Kaunaz appears in the inverted position. You may feel yourself to be adrift, abandoned, and with little idea of what to do next. However, Kaunaz is primarily associated with learning, so it is important to remember that some lessons are hard ones. It may be that it is time to let go of the past and to move on. All will be revealed in time, so don't panic. The lessons that you need to learn will become evident to you and you will soon find the right path, even if the guiding light of Kaunaz seems dimmed at the moment.

Gebo

"Gyfu brings credit and honor which support one's dignity, it fur-nishes help and subsistence to all broken men, devoid of aught else."

"THE ANGLO-SAXON RUNE POEM"

AALTERNATIVE NAMES

This rune was Gyfu to the ancient Anglo-Saxons.

PRONUNCIATION

"G."

KEY CONCEPTS

Gifts, generosity, and help for those who are in need are signified by Gebo. Gebo is also said to indicate love, perhaps in the more general sense of charity rather than the pure-ly personal. Oxen make an appearance with Gebo because cattle were the measure of wealth among the early peoples of Northern Europe. Another concept intimately connect-ed with that of generosity is that of boundary markers. In other words, being overly gener-ous can also be a bad thing. In addition, recognizing one's own boundaries is as important as knowing how much to give. In another sense, the rune is connected with innate talents, or abilities that can be taken as gifts from the gods.

This is the first rune of the series not to have an inverted meaning, so its message must be taken at face value.

In reflection of the beliefs of early Northern European peoples, herds of cattle symbolize the wealth, harmony, and generosity associated with the gift-giving rune, Gebo.

MYTHOLOGY

Both Odin and Thor are symbolically associated with Gebo. Its significance of knowing one's boundaries and swearing to abide by contracts link the rune with Thor, the thunder god whose job it was to preserve order in the universe. Odin, being the archetypal king, was expected to give generous gifts to his followers in order to reward them for their loyalty. He possessed a marvelous armring called Draupnir, which replicated itself into eight other, identical rings every ninth night. These precious objects were then distributed as it pleased him. Gebo has thus gained an extra interpretation as a valuable ornament. In his song, Odin warns that "It is better not to ask than to overpledge, as a gift demands a gift." This verse speaks both of making hasty promises and of casting enchantments. In both cases, a price must be paid, so caution should be the watchword.

The giving and receiving of gifts is the main symbolic meaning of Gebo. However, the "Song of Odin" warns that "It is better not to ask than to overpledge."

MEANING

The giving and receiving of gifts has been important in every society. As a gesture of mutual respect and a symbol of fondness, the custom is meant to bind people together. This may be why we still mark affectionate letters with an "X" to denote a kiss, while in previous ages, when most people were illiterate, documents were signed with an "X" to signify an acceptance of a contract or agreement. Bringing the aspect of relationship to the fore, Gebo signifies both the donor and the recipient of a gift. All should be well as long as there are conditions and both parties know the limits of their agreement, even if nothing material is actually given. The payment for the gift may come in the form of simple gratitude, but if that is withheld, then resentment and quarrels will be the result. The same applies to the giver: a present should be given with an

open heart, otherwise the giver will feel forced into an obligation and the recipient will feel worthless.

When Gebo appears, it is certain that you will feel honor-bound to help someone out very soon. However, it is important to judge exactly how much help you should give. After all, if you are too generous, then this needy person may become overly reliant upon you; if you are not generous enough, however, you could be considered a skinflint and your reputation could suffer.

Odin's birds, a pair of harness mounts from Gotland. The exaggerated beaks and talons emphasise the ferocity of the eagles that were widely associated with the cult of Odin. (Viking, Sweden.)

Wunjo

"He lives well who knows not suffering, sorrow, nor anxiety, and has prosperity and happiness and a good enough house."

"THE ANGLO-SAXON RUNE POEM"

ALTERNATIVE NAMES

To the Anglo-Saxons, this rune was known as Wynn.

PRONUNCIATION

"W" or "V."

KEY CONCEPTS

Perfection, harmony, domestic bliss, a happy household, good fortune, and trusted friends are denoted by Wunjo. Beauty, fair skin, and fine hair are also traditionally linked to this rune. It is said to be one of the four runes of love and suggests an attraction that will blossom into a lasting relationship. The rune is airy in nature, with associations with clouds, the wind, spinning wheels, and flax.

The romantic rune Wunjo represents good fortune, happy endings, weddings, and lasting love.

MYTHOLOGY

The dutiful Frigga, the wife of Odin and queen of the gods of Asgard, is the main deity associated with this rune. This goddess was the epitome of wifely virtues, who sat at her spinning wheel creating the clouds. In Southern Germany, she was said to be shaking the fluff off her blankets if the sky was full of misty vapor. She was the patroness of all of the domestic arts and, like many a mortal lady, was a true romantic at heart, with a soft spot for lovers and happy endings. Frigga can be regarded as the model for the fairy godmother found in so many children's stories – the kindly lady who makes it work out all right in the end. This aspect of the goddess, and, indeed, her wish-granting husband, is found in the name of the Anglo-Saxon version of the rune, Wynn. This word has survived in modern English as the verb "to win," while Wunjo is the origin of the verb "to woo." This connection with wooing makes Frigga the archetypal matronly matchmaker, eternally ensuring that Cinderella marries her Prince Charming and that they live happily ever after.

The Germanic peoples believed that clouds were created by Odin's wife, Frigga, as she worked at her spinning wheel.

UPRIGHT MEANING

Absolute love, the arrival of good news, an excellent turn of fortune, and the establishment of a happy home. All in all, Wunjo represents a fulfilling life or, at the very least, a period when everything will go your way. Partnerships, of course, are of prime importance when this rune appears, not only relationships of an emotional nature, but those connected with business, too. Firm friendships and mutually advantageous arrangements are under the auspices of this rune. But it is in the realm of love that Wunjo truly shines. If you are unattached, someone attractive is likely suddenly to walk into your life. Tradition states that this person is likely to be pale-skinned and fair-haired, but we must remember that these characteristics were the ancient Norse measures of beauty and that they did not live in a multicultural society. Artistic or other creative ventures will be successful, and you may receive news from a distance, probably from a man who has journeyed over water. In health terms, the appearance of Wunjo shows that some tender loving care will pay off and that a recovery is likely.

INVERTED MEANING

Trust becomes an issue when Wunjo is inverted. Prospective partners may not be all that they seem, so don't give your heart too readily. In business, too, beware of double-dealing and don't take anything at face value. If at all possible, delay making far-reaching judgements as you will not have all of the facts that you need to make a valid decision. Tradition says that if you have an emotional worry you should delay your decision-making for three months. If the troublesome factor is in business, put off any action for three days. Things will slow down for a while and you may become despondent about your prospects.

THE SECOND SEQUENCE: Hagel's Aett

The runes of the second sequence take their name from the first rune to appear. This is Hagalaz, so this sequence could be described as the aett of hail or inclement weather. The order of the runes in this sequence is as follows: Hagalaz, Nauthiz, Isa, Jera, Eihwaz, Pertho, Algiz, and, finally, Sowelo.

After the perfection achieved at the end of the first sequence, the runes now show a darker face, and the forces of disruption make their presence felt with the

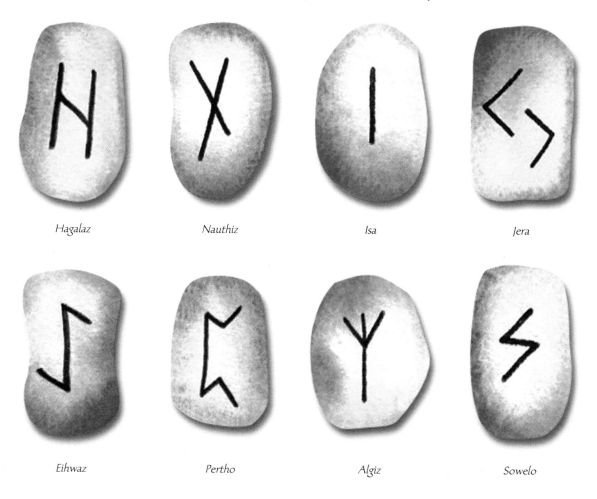

Hagalaz	*Nauthiz*	*Isa*	*Jera*
Eihwaz	*Pertho*	*Algiz*	*Sowelo*

first three runes of the second aett. Hagalaz, Nauthiz, and Isa mean hail, necessity, and ice respectively, but behind the troubles that these bring lie the workings of fate, personified by the three Norns, the weavers of the web of Wyrd. These runes are also known as the runes of cold. However, after these trials, there is rejoicing, symbolized by Jera, which also signifies midwinter and the Yuletide season. This is the lowest point of the Sun's passage through the year, and from now on the days gradually begin to become longer, as denoted by the rune Eihwaz. Pertho, the rune of birth, follows, signaling the promise of spring, when desire flourishes, symbolized by Algiz (in runic astrology, Algiz covers the period that we now mark with St. Valentine's Day). The last rune

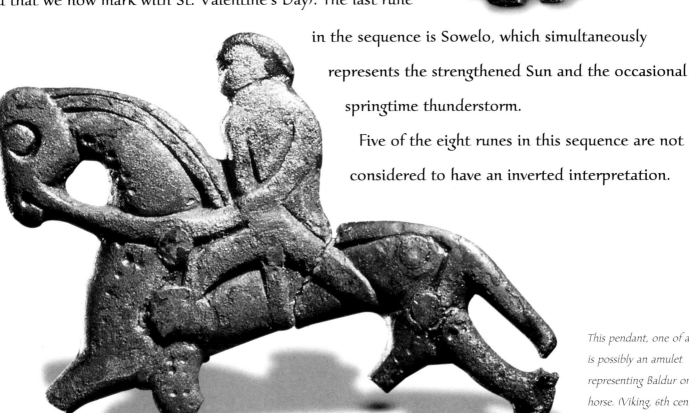

A pendant, usually identified as a Valkyrie.

in the sequence is Sowelo, which simultaneously represents the strengthened Sun and the occasional springtime thunderstorm.

Five of the eight runes in this sequence are not considered to have an inverted interpretation.

This pendant, one of a pair, is possibly an amulet representing Baldur on his horse. (Viking, 6th century, Sweden.)

Hagalaz

"Hagall is the whitest of grain, it is whirled from the vault of heaven and tossed about by gusts of wind then melts into water."

"THE ANGLO-SAXON RUNE POEM"

"Hagall is cold grain and driving sleet and the sickness a serpent brings."

"THE ICELANDIC RUNE POEM"

ALTERNATIVE NAMES

To the Anglo-Saxons, this rune was known as Heagl. The Norse spoke of it as Hagall.

PRONUNCIATION

"H."

KEY CONCEPTS

The words Hagalaz, Hagall, and Heagl literally mean "hail" or "sleet," as hinted at in the words of the Anglo-Saxon and Icelandic rune poems above. The rune thus suggests cold winds and bad weather. Since the ancient Norse people were great travelers, especially by sea, such weather conditions were not only disruptive, but very dangerous. Indeed, one of their poetic descriptions of the ocean was the "cold, gray widow-maker." Likewise, the appearance of Hagalaz foretells a blast of disruption sweeping through our lives. The rune is also associated with other potential misfortunes, such as the venom of a serpent.

The rune Hagalaz represents difficulty and peril, especially when traveling over water. To emphasize the point, the Vikings called the sea the "cold, gray widow-maker."

MYTHOLOGY

The runes of the second aett take their name from Hagalaz. The first aett begins with chaos and continues to describe the order that was created from it. In this case, the chaos is unexpected, although it is intimately connected with the past. The goddess most closely associated with Hagalaz is Urd, one of the three Norns who wove the web of fate. Urd was thought to be the Norn of the past, the other two, Verdandi and Skuld, being the present and future respectively. Another, more sinister, goddess is also connected with this rune. She is Hel, or Hella, from whose name we derive the English word "hell." A hideous apparition, Hel was thought to be a moldering corpse on the right side of her face and body, yet a beautiful woman on the left. This dreadful goddess was the ruler of the world of the dishonored dead. The guardian of roads and passageways between the worlds, the watchful Heimdall also has an association with this rune. Interestingly, in runic astrology, Hagalaz is said to represent Hallowe'en.

Hagalaz is the rune of desperate confusion and the fear of the unknown.

UPRIGHT MEANING

This is the rune of the unknown, of frightening and mysterious events. Sudden, disruptive things are about to occur and your life will be turned on its head for a while. You will have very little power to avert these happenings, which, like cold, Arctic winds, will blow hard and confuse your senses with swirling sleet. This meaning could be taken quite literally as a disruption to travel plans due to inclement weather conditions, but it is more likely that its interpretation goes beyond the merely literal. It is fortunate that the cold winds of icy reality that are set to blow will soon yield to the softer breezes of spring, so hope is implicit in the meaning of Hagalaz. All that you have to do is to sit out the storm and make sure that you wrap up warm. Hagalaz is also considered to be the rune of gamblers,

especially those who risk a lot. Since it is the ninth in the Elder Futhark series, it has a correspondence with the number nine.

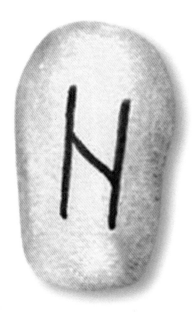

INVERTED MEANING

Many rune readers do not consider Hagalaz to have an inverted meaning: it is always a disruptive and uncomfortable influence. However, if this rune repeatedly occurs in the inverted position, then there is a danger of silly, avoidable accidents. In this case, the rune suggests that more forethought would be a very good idea. Take your time, don't rush, and think through each of your moves very carefully indeed.

Nauthiz

"Nyd is oppressive to the heart yet often proves a help and is the salvation of the children of men who heed it in time."

"THE ANGLO-SAXON RUNE POEM"

ALTERNATIVE NAMES

To the Anglo-Saxons, this rune was known as Nyd, while in Scandinavia it was called Naudr, which became Naud in Iceland. All of these words mean "need."

PRONUNCIATION

"N."

KEY CONCEPTS

This is the rune of necessity, as its very name means "need." As the words of the rune poem say, that which is necessary is often "oppressive to the heart," but it can be a great teacher about the reality of the world and our place within it. Of course, managing life often relies upon a little good luck, and it is possible that the custom of crossing one's fingers harkens back to the shape of the rune Nauthiz. This rune also has associations with the so-called "need-fires" that were lit in times of plague or famine, and with rowan and beech trees, too.

A brooch in the form of the world serpent. (Viking, 7th century, Sweden.)

The need for luck that is symbolized by the rune Nauthiz gives it an association with the beech tree, which was considered to be fortunate.

MYTHOLOGY

Nauthiz is connected with one of the Norns, the goddesses of fate: with Skuld, the veiled Norn of the future, who assures us through this rune that what must be, must be. Skuld was considered to be the youngest of the three goddesses of fate, and as the Norn of the hidden future she is particularly important to divination. On a less positive note, the rune is also associated with the dreadful serpent Nidhog, whose name literally means "gnawer from beneath." This monster endlessly assaults the roots of the world tree that is the backbone of the cosmos. The rune can be regarded as symbolic of fear or insecurity undermining personal self-confidence, just as its mythical counterpart constantly attempts to subvert the order of the universe. Just as the previous rune, Hagalaz, is connected to one of the nine worlds of Norse mythology, so Nauthiz, too, governs a plane of existence. It is said that the serpent Nidhog resides in a place called Nifelhel. This is where hopes are dashed; feelings of failure are overwhelming; and despair is a crushing weight. It is little wonder, then, that in such a state a little of the luck of Nauthiz is a welcome gift.

UPRIGHT MEANING

This rune is likely to appear when you are assailed by doubt and insecurity. Indeed, it indicates that you should think very carefully before acting. A realistic attitude is vital, but it is also important to remember that realism is not equated with pessimism. Nauthiz is fundamentally the rune of necessity, so some action is required of you, no matter how much anxiety and lack of confidence may hamper your activities. Strength of character and a determination to control these negative emotions will see you through this period. Another aspect of the rune is the importance of recognizing your own limitations and acting accordingly. Pushing yourself too hard will solve little at this time. Irritation with your limitations may make you intolerant of the fail-

ings of others, too. Although the period forecast by Nauthiz is not likely to be pleasant, good will come out of it. Luck is waiting around the corner, and good fortune is particularly likely to come from older relatives and true friends, who will stick by you through thick and thin.

INVERTED MEANING

The frustrations and stress of the upright Nauthiz are even more evident when the rune is inverted. The Norn of the future seems more heavily veiled than usual, and you will find it difficult to anticipate forthcoming events. You may lack a clear sense of direction and so may be easily led into taking unwise actions. Beware of get-rich-quick schemes and false friends. On the other hand, the appearance of the inverted Nauthiz may simply be an indication that the answer to your question is at present unknown . . . even to the runes!

Isa

"Ice is too cold and slippery, it shines like glass and is most like to gems. A floor wrought by frost fair to see."

"THE ANGLO-SAXON RUNE POEM"

ALTERNATIVE NAMES

To the Vikings, this rune was known as Is; to the Icelanders, Iss; and to the ancient Teutons, Isa, which literally means "ice."

PRONUNCIATION

"EE," as in "even."

KEY CONCEPTS

The shape of this rune represents an icicle: cold, hard, unyielding, and capable of causing pain when grasped. By extension, ice in general is associated with the rune, especially the type of ice that makes walking difficult. It is connected with the slow-moving, inexorable glacier, too. Being notable for its hardness, Isa is also associated with the cold iron from which weapons are made. The symbolic beasts associated with Isa are the herds of reindeer that roam the snowy wastes, as well as ferocious wild boars. The vegetable symbols of Isa include the alder tree and the poisonous herb henbane. The rune is also connected with the number seven.

MYTHOLOGY

Verdandi, the Norn of the present, is the third goddess of fate to appear in this sequence of runes. Her iron will as guardian of the status quo fits perfectly with the nature of Isa. Another goddess whose cold heart resisted warmth and persuasion of all kinds is Rind, who refused Odin the means to avenge the death of his son. Rind is symbolic of the frozen earth of winter.

MEANING

Like the infinitely slow-moving glacier, the force of the rune Isa is unstoppable. All you require when this rune is found in a reading is that rarest of virtues, patience. The appearance of Isa is most distressing when a question is asked about relationships, because this icy rune foretells a period of emotional cooling. Yet this is not necessarily a permanent state of affairs, because a thaw will eventually come and the ice will melt. In other affairs, Isa also slows events down to a crawl. Business partnerships may go through a rocky patch because expected events will not happen when they are supposed to. You may also find that any blocks to your ambitions will turn out to be disguised blessings because your aims

The slow, inexorable movement of a glacier represents the unstoppable change that is part of the rune of Isa's meaning.

The vast herds of reindeer that roam the snowy, northern wastes are numbered among the animals that symbolize the rune Isa.

and desires will change during the period of the delay.

Even though this rune is not the most comfortable to live with, and can be most distressing for affairs of the heart, the cool clarity of ice bestows a calmness conducive to quiet contemplation. The true gift of Isa is a respite from cluttered thinking, which will allow you to see your situation and prospects more clearly. It may even show you how to progress in the future to avoid the pitfalls and slipups that would otherwise occur.

If you are involved in a creative venture of any kind, it would be a good idea to take a pause from it. Even if you believe that you are wasting time, nothing could be farther from the truth. This interval will allow you to recharge your talents , and when the thaw sets in you will thus be able to pursue your tasks with renewed vigor.

Traditionally, the rune Isa is associated with the number seven, so its appearance as a final rune could indicate a period of seven days. If it falls in the middle of a reading, it is said to emphasize the message of the other runes.

Isa is said to have no inverted meaning. However, if you do choose to interpret it in the reversed position, the immobility that it suggests can be taken as a message that you can go no farther and must completely change your direction.

In order to survive the harsh conditions of the bleak, icy tundras of the Arctic regions, patience and determination are required.

Jera

"Jera is a joy to men when the gods make the earth to bring forth shining fruits for rich and poor alike."

"THE ANGLO-SAXON RUNE POEM"

ALTERNATIVE NAMES

This rune was also called Jer by the Anglo-Saxons of Northumbria, England, and Ar by both the Norwegians and Icelanders.

PRONUNCIATION

"J" or "Y."

KEY CONCEPTS

Jera is connected with the yearly cycle of nature, particularly with the harvest and the celebrations that go with it. It is also symbolized by the strength of the venerable oak and the humble herb rosemary. It is a rune of joy, of plenty, and of rich blessings. Jera's association with celebration connects it with Yuletide, or our Christmas season, and it expresses much of the warmth and happiness of this time. In this sense, Jera is symbolically assigned the winter solstice, when the Sun is at its weakest, yet begins to gain strength once more. Jera is the twelfth rune and therefore the halfway point of the Elder Futhark. The year also has twelve months, and in ancient times the day was in addition held to consist of twelve hours.

The humble herb rosemary symbolizes the joy associated with Jera, the rune of celebration.

The brightly decorated Christmas tree is the most familiar aspect of the rune Jera. Its image evokes happy memories and the Yuletide spirit.

MYTHOLOGY

The symbolism of Jera relates to the tragic tale of Baldur and Hodur, two of the sons of Odin. Baldur, who was known as "the Beautiful," shone like the Sun. Poor Hodur, on the other hand, was blind and so quiet that he was often ignored. Baldur was so beloved of both gods and humans that his mother, Frigga, spent a long time extracting a promise from every living thing that they would not harm him. However, she ignored the mistletoe because it was so puny that she could not imagine that it could possibly hurt her beloved son. Unfortunately, Frigga had not considered the malice of the deceitful fire god, Loki. Loki incited the other gods to throw weapons at Baldur, all of which bounced off him. Then he suggested other objects, such as pots and pans. No harm came to Baldur. Only blind Hodur held back because he could not see his brother, but wily Loki persuaded him to join in the game and offered not only to guide his hand, but to provide him with an unlikely weapon: a dart made from the puny mistletoe. This small dart alone hit its mark, and Baldur fell down dead, slain by his brother's hand. But all was not lost, for Baldur eventually conquered death and was later resurrected, just like the Sun on midwinter's day.

MEANING

Jera is connected with endings and new beginnings. Its presence in a reading predicts a time when your present trials will end and you can make a fresh, optimistic start. The rune's association with the harvest also associates Jera with the concept of reaping the rewards of your past efforts. Its appearance signifies a completion of some project, which will be celebrated with joy and relief. Jera shows that your optimism will not be misplaced and that personal success is very likely. A new home or the signing of contracts is also suggested by the rune. It may be that you will have to employ the services of a professional person, such as a lawyer or an accountant, to put the final seal on an advantageous agreement of some kind.

Jera's connection with the number twelve may suggest that a period of twelve months or a year is indicated. This need not necessarily mean that you will have to wait a year for the good times to come again, just that the abundant good luck of the rune may last a considerable period, such as twelve months. After all, it may take some time and effort to reach the successful conclusion that you desire.

Like the preceding rune, Isa, Jera has no inverted interpretation.

The Christmas period isn't the only celebration associated with Jera: the harvest festival that follows the reaping of abundant crops is also symbolized by this rune.

Eihwaz

"Eoh is a tree with rough bark, hard and fast in the earth, supported by its roots."

"THE ANGLO-SAXON RUNE POEM"

ALTERNATIVE NAMES

The rune Eihwaz was known as Eoh to the Anglo-Saxons.

PRONUNCIATION

"Y," or alternatively, "E," as in "ever."

KEY CONCEPTS

Most of the concepts associated with Eihwaz relate to trees. The rune is said to symbolize variously the apple tree, the poplar, and the yew. The latter identification seems to be the most potent, because it was from the yew that bows were made. The yew is often found in the vicinity of graveyards, so it becomes a symbol of the past growing into the future. It is probably also connected with Yggdrasil, the "world tree," the backbone of the universe. Eihwaz is another rune associated with horses, too, especially the mighty Sleipnir, the eight-legged steed of Odin. The herb bryony is the vegetable symbol of the rune.

The yew tree was often planted in graveyards to symbolize the growing of the past into the future.

MYTHOLOGY

Ullr, the great hunter and wanderer of the northern wastelands, is the god connected with this rune. A sure shot with his yew bow, Ullr was accustomed to taking risks. It is even claimed that he once impersonated and replaced Odin as king of the gods of Asgard for a while. More usually, Ullr lived in a place called Ydalir, the "valley of the yews," when he was not out terrorizing wildlife with his bow. The myth of Ullr's replacement of Odin is very ancient. It may be that both gods were considered to be two sides of the same coin, Odin governing the summer months and Ullr the winter. The legend of a wild huntsman careering through the skies of Northern Europe survived beyond the Middle Ages and entered the folklore of many countries.

Eihwaz is connected with horses, especially Sleipnir, the steed of Odin that could gallop across the foamy sea and over a field of wheat without bending a single stalk.

MEANING

The appearance of Eihwaz in a reading indicates progress. Even if your life seems to be moving at a snail's pace, a new situation will soon manifest itself and events will speed up so much that you may find it difficult to keep track of everything. You'll need to pay close attention to happenings around you to keep up. Adaptability and a readiness to make a speedy decision will be vital if you are to make the most of this positive rune. Eihwaz is closely associated with hunting skills, so you must act as though you were an archer of old: wait until your target is in your sights and then, when the moment is right, strike out for it. Don't worry that you may miss your moment, or, indeed, miss the target: you have the acumen and shrewdness to choose the correct time and to act boldly when the occasion arises. Eihwaz shows that bravery has every indication of success.

This rune encourages you to gather your courage and take a risk. Its message is one of "nothing ventured, nothing gained," and now is the time to take action. Eihwaz is thus considered to be a lucky rune for gamblers and those who live by their wits. Its appearance in a reading may show the positive influence of a strong-willed person, especially a woman.

Another good aspect of Eihwaz is that, under its influence, expected problems will not arise. The rune also indicates long-term benefits, even if you have to put up with an uncomfortable or stressful situation for a short while. Eihwaz is said to be a beneficial indicator for students and is also held to dispel storms and to calm tempestuous emotions.

Eihwaz has no inverted meaning.

The huntsman Ullr was a master of the yew bow whose arrow never failed to find its mark.

Pertho

"Peoro is a source of recreation and amusement to the great, where warriors sit blithely together in the banquet hall."

"THE ANGLO-SAXON RUNE POEM"

ALTERNATIVE NAMES

To the Anglo-Saxons, this rune was known as Peoro.

PRONUNCIATION

"P."

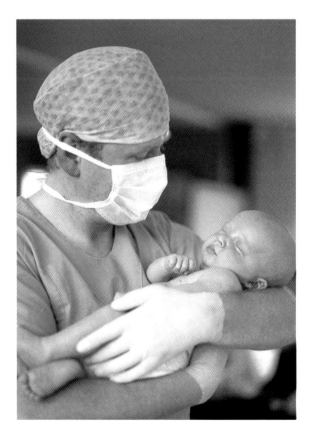

KEY CONCEPTS

As the words of the rune poem above indicate, this rune is primarily associated with mysteries and the amusement that results from their revelation. However, there is reason to believe that this part of the poem is a mistranslation, and that it is the wives of the warriors, and not the warriors, who take such joy in the revelation of secrets. On this feminine note, Pertho is connected with birth and death, and thus with beginnings and endings of all kinds. The mysteries of the occult, and of what lies before and after life, are related ideas. Another side to the rune is its association with gaming, and the very shape of the rune suggests a dice cup. The word "Pertho" is said to mean a pawn or gaming piece, so playing the game, and winning and losing, are powerful concepts relating to this fateful rune.

The mysterious rune Pertho is intimately connected with the Norns, the weavers of the web of fate. The rune symbolizes both the beginning and the end of life.

MYTHOLOGY

Games of chance and skill are jointly governed by all three of the goddesses of fate, the Norns. This goes for life, too, the greatest game of chance and skill of all. In Norse mythology, these eternally weaving, enigmatic goddesses were not forthcoming with their knowledge and had to be wooed to reveal the future. Even Odin himself had to resort to outrageous bribery to find out what the web of Wyrd had in store. Although Odin had little influence with the weavers of the web, the same cannot be said for his wife, Frigga. This paragon of domestic virtue seems to have been on very good terms with them, and was additionally regarded as the patroness of women in labor. Frigga was also believed to be the mother of at least some of the Valkyries, the warrior women who rode flying steeds over battlefields to select those who had died bravely to enjoy a happy afterlife in the hall of their father, Odin.

Pertho is said to resemble a dice cup. Games of chance and skill are indicated by the appearance of this enigmatic runic symbol.

UPRIGHT MEANING

If Pertho is the first, or, indeed, the only, rune of your reading, then stop immediately. The rune is telling you that you are not meant to know the answer to your question at this time. Any foreknowledge on your part would change the pattern of the web of Wyrd, and the Norns will not divulge any information that would jeopardize their hard work. However, if Pertho appears in the middle, or at the end, of a reading, then kindly fate is taking a hand in your affairs and a celebration is in the offing. Problems will be solved, your knowledge will increase, and you will find emotional security in good company. The rune suggests that you are playing the game of life well, and that you are definitely on a winning streak. Prophetic dreams are associated with this aspect of Pertho, too. There may also

be news of a birth, a new enterprise, or, indeed, any event that will transform your life and how you live it. One word of caution: because Pertho is associated with secrets, use any information that comes you way with discretion. It wouldn't do to reveal your hand before you have made your play.

INVERTED MEANING

Fate can deal a crushing blow when Pertho is inverted in a reading. The pattern of fate takes on a darker hue and the game of life will transform the board into something rather frightening and unfamiliar. Perhaps you have overestimated your chances of success and have overplayed your hand. There are facts that you are unaware of, however, so proceed cautiously, gamble nothing, and wait until the Norns are in a better humor.

Algiz

"Secg is mostly found in marshes, it grows in water and inflicts a terrible wound. The blood burns in every man who grasps it."

"THE ANGLO-SAXON RUNE POEM"

ALTERNATIVE NAMES

In some parts of England, the Anglo-Saxons called this rune Secg, although it was more commonly called Eolh.

PRONUNCIATION

Usually a long "Z," as in "buzz," but occasionally "R," or even "M," although there are other runes that represent these sounds.

KEY CONCEPTS

This is another rune that is symbolically connected with the mighty elk, as well as the yew tree. It is, however, also associated with the lime tree and with semiaquatic plants, such as reeds, rushes, eelgrass, and sedge. The form of the rune resembles an outstretched hand, probably representing the hand of Tyr, which was sacrificed for the safety of the universe (see Tiwaz, page 77). It also looks like the outstretched branches of a tree or the footprint of a bird, such as a crow or raven. The upright position of this rune was used to denote the date of birth on Viking tombstones. The inverted form was likewise used to give the date of death.

The Valkyries, the warrior daughters of Odin, were said sometimes to take the form of crows in order to haunt fields of battle. The shape of the Algiz rune may represent the footprint of the crow.

The shape of the rune Algiz reminded some northern peoples of the antlers of the mighty elk.

MYTHOLOGY

The deities primarily associated with Algiz are the Valkyries, the shape-shifting warrior women. These daughters of Odin were the protectors of brave men in battle, but also chose the most suitable candidates for a seat at their father's table in Valhalla after their deaths. Accomplished in magic, the Valkyries often took the forms of carrion birds when carrying out their grim business. The footprint of these birds may be the origin of the shape of this rune. The brooding watchman of the gods, Heimdall, is also connected with Algiz because he, in his form as a beacon or watch-tower, is symbolic of the illumination that Algiz can give.

UPRIGHT MEANING

Algiz is the supreme rune for healing and protection. In ancient magic, it was said that the power of Algiz could protect not only oneself, but one's family and friends, too. Bearing this in mind, the appearance of Algiz in a reading suggests that there will be a successful outcome to an endeavor, that a health problem will be overcome, and that help will be given to you by a caring friend. Although this is a rune of self-interest, it does not denote selfishness. Its main message is that you should make time for yourself and hold on to your dreams and desires. The demands of others should be a secondary consideration, because if you don't look after yourself, then you will be in no position to look after anyone else in the future. Any creative ventures are favored by the appearance of Algiz. You may take up a new and therapeutic hobby and delve into fascinating areas that have previously escaped your notice. Algiz is also a rune of meditation, and the message of its surrounding runes in a reading may point the way to personal illumination of some kind.

INVERTED MEANING

In the inverted position, this rune reinforces the message of its upright meaning. It can show that health problems are occurring, or will occur very soon, and that you need to concern yourself with your own welfare. However, other people may refuse to recognize that you are overburdened and weary. The demands of these folk will not cease, because when Algiz is inverted, you will find that those around you are very insensitive indeed. While in this low state, you will be somewhat weak-willed and will tend to agree to anything simply to have some peace. You should bear this in mind and slow down. Go into retreat and seclusion and don't take on anything more just yet. Algiz signals a period of recuperation, so allow yourself the time to regain your strength.

Sowelo

"Sol is the shield of the sky and shining rays and destroyer of ice."

"THE ANGLO-SAXON RUNE POEM"

ALTERNATIVE NAMES

This rune was known as Sol to the Norse and as Sigil to the Anglo-Saxons of Northumbria.

PRONUNCIATION

"S."

KEY CONCEPTS

Sowelo is the rune of the Sun, expressing the brightness, fertility, and good fortune associated with that heavenly orb. It speaks of the life force and of the urge to grow that is found in all living things. Sowelo's symbols include the soaring eagle, the venerable oak tree, and also the juniper and bay trees. Mistletoe, which is also associated with the twelfth rune, Jera, is another potent symbol of the Sun. The shape of the rune suggests a flash of lightning descending to earth, an association that brings the formidable power of the mighty god of thunder, Thor, into the interpretation of the Sowelo rune.

Sowelo, the rune of the Sun, is symbolically associated with another king of the sky: the soaring eagle.

The awesome lightning flash signifies Thor's power to smite down wrongdoers. Sowelo ensures that people receive their just rewards for good or evil deeds.

MYTHOLOGY

In northern mythology, the Sun is considered to be female, personified as a giantess named either Sol or Sunna. Two of the Asgardian deities are also associated with this rune. The first is Baldur, "the Beautiful," the beloved, yet tragic, god, who was slain by a mistletoe dart thrown by his blind brother, Hodur. This myth expresses the cycle of the year and the duality of light and darkness. The thunder god, Thor, must have a place in the symbolism of the rune, because it looks so much like a lightning flash. Thor, the guardian of justice and order, was known for the swift retribution that he dealt out to wrongdoers. So the meaning of this rune can be applied to the workings of the law and also to taking justified revenge.

MEANING

In the harsh northern world, the Sun was beloved by all. Sowelo is thus primarily a rune of love. Its appearance in a reading casts a warm glow over all of the other runes present and undoes much of the harm that they may foretell. It is also a rune of hope, promising that the Sun will rise once more, even when one is in the darkest night. It is a particularly good rune to draw when one is in trouble, because it will ensure a happy outcome. One might also say that Sowelo expresses the idea of poetic justice, because it indicates that wrongdoers will gain nothing but an apt punishment for their offenses.

If you have a major decision to make, then the appearance of Sowelo will reveal the truth of the situation, making your choice easier. There is a spiritual dimension to this rune, too, and when it is drawn, contact with your inner self will guide you.

In affairs of the heart, this rune is a good omen. Thor, one of the patron deities of Sowelo, was invoked at weddings in Viking times, when brides wore red, the color of Thor, and held the god's symbol, the hammer, as the vows were exchanged.

Sowelo signals a time when happiness and harmony will reign and justice will prevail. The rune's association with the Sun may also hint at an enjoyable holiday. It is also said to be a good sign of victory in athletics or sport.

Sowelo has no inverted interpretation.

like the sunrise, the appearance of Sowelo casts a warm glow over other runes in the reading. Sowelo is a good rune to draw when one is in trouble.

THE THIRD SEQUENCE:
Tyr's Aett

The runes of the third sequence tend to refer to humankind and earthly things. More specifically, many of the runes of this aett are directly associated with human society and customs and domesticated animals and plants. As usual, this aett begins with the rune that gives it its name: Tyr, or Tiwaz. This rune is masculine and signifies the male principle, including honor and trust in human

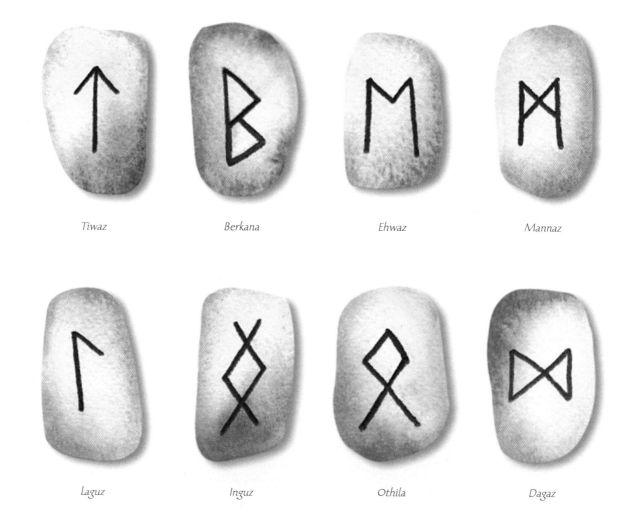

Tiwaz   Berkana   Ehwaz   Mannaz

Laguz   Inguz   Othila   Dagaz

society. Berkana follows next, symbolizing women and fertility, trees and plants. Ehwaz is the rune of horses and domesticated animals; Mannaz symbolizes the union of men and women and represents humankind in general. Laguz, the rune of water, is connected with safe harbors, ships, and fishing. Inguz denotes offspring and the principle of inheritance. Othila stands for kingship, nobility, and government; and, finally, Dagaz, the rune of midsummer, completes the sequence with joyous celebration.

The "bound devil" on a cross at Kirkby Stephen, Cumbria. Loki is shown fettered after contriving Baldur's death. In Scandinavian mythology, Loki was the embodiment of deceit and trickery. (Viking, c. 1000 A.D., England.)

The Andreas Stone, with a relief depicting a scene from the legendary Norse poem, "Ragnarok," in which the god Odin is eaten by the wolf Fenris. (Viking, England.)

Tiwaz

"Tiw is a guiding star, well does it keep faith with princes. It is ever on course over the mists of night and never fails."

"THE ANGLO-SAXON RUNE POEM"

"Tyr is one-handed among the gods and leavings of wolf and king of temples."

"THE ICELANDIC RUNE POEM"

ALTERNATIVE NAMES

Tiwaz is also given as Teiwaz. To the Norse of Scandinavia and Iceland, the rune was known as Tyr, while to the Saxons it was Tiw.

PRONUNCIATION

"T."

KEY CONCEPTS

This rune is symbolically connected with the North Star, which "never fails," and with vows and unbreakable oaths. The custom of holding up one's right hand while taking an oath is derived from the story of Tyr (see below). The trees of Tiwaz are the mighty oak and the hazel. The spear is also a symbol of Tiwaz, as might be expected, since the rune represents the god of war. The shape of the rune suggests the unvarying compass needle, too.

Tiwaz represents the Northern Star, whose symbolic virtue is, that like the compass, its needle unfailingly points north. This rune therefore provides infallible guidance.

The oak tree was considered sacred to the king of the gods in many mythologies. The fact that it is associated with the god Tiw is an indication that it was he, rather than Odin, who was thought to be the monarch of the northern pantheon.

MYTHOLOGY

Tiwaz is an ancient name for the god of war and justice, who was first mentioned by the Roman writer Tacitus, who claimed that Tiwaz was the king of the Germanic gods. When this role was later assumed by Odin, Tiwaz took a humbler form as the god Tyr. To the Saxons, he was known as Tiw, and it is from his name that we derive our word "Tuesday." His most famous story involves a monstrous wolf called Fenris, who had grown so large that he threatened to devour the whole universe to satisfy his ravenous hunger. The gods tried to bind the monster with ropes and chains, but these proved to be no restraint to Fenris, who broke them with a shrug. Eventually, one of the dwarf craftsmen made an enchanted ribbon that was as fine as a woman's hair and swore that this alone would be strong enough to fetter the beast. However, scenting magic, the wolf refused to allow the gods to bind him. Then brave Tyr stepped forward and offered to place his right hand in the mouth of the monster as a guarantee that all would be well. To the relief of the gods, the binding held and the Fenris wolf was imprisoned. Now the monster took his revenge by biting off Tyr's extended hand, which was nobly sacrificed for the good of all.

UPRIGHT MEANING

Binding oaths are indicated by Tiwaz. This may seem paradoxical, since Tiwaz broke his oath to the wolf, yet that oath was made under duress and he had good reason to lie. A worthy promise, made under the right conditions and for honorable reasons, should, and, indeed, must, be kept. Marriage vows are a case in point. Tiwaz is thought to signify lasting love, and its appearance denotes a bond that, once made, cannot be broken. However, Tiwaz is also an aggressively masculine rune, so it tends to favor men rather than the women. Any relationship question that is answered by Tiwaz shows that passions will run riot because two strong-minded people will be involved. While sex will never be boring, the danger of jealousy will always be present. If the person asking the question is a woman, Tiwaz suggests that a strong and handsome man will love her fiercely and that she may have to sacrifice something major in

her life to ensure that her attachment to him remains strong. However, once that has been done, the relationship will prosper. Love will be steadfast, or, as Shakespeare described it, "as constant as the Northern Star."

Tiwaz also indicates success in business and sports. It suggests that legal decisions will go in your favor, too. In these matters, as in affairs of the heart, an unshakeable conviction that what you are doing is right will give you the strength of purpose to succeed.

INVERTED MEANING

Selfishness, dishonorable actions and turning one's back on responsibilities are suggested when Tiwaz is inverted. Women should not trust their men so readily, because in this position the rune often denotes a shallow relationship.

Berkana

"Beorc bears no fruit, yet without seed it brings forth shoots, for it is generated from its leaves. Splendid are its branches and gloriously adorned, its lofty crown reaching the sky."

"THE ANGLO-SAXON RUNE POEM"

ALTERNATIVE NAMES

To the Anglo-Saxons, the rune was Beorc, while to the Norse of Scandinavia and Iceland it was known as Bjarkan.

PRONUNCIATION

"B."

KEY CONCEPTS

This rune is feminine in nature and has connotations of motherhood, domesticity, and protectiveness, seen in the shape of the rune, which suggests breasts. Its animal symbols include the she bear and the graceful swan. In human terms, wise women, herbalists, and healers are also indicated by the rune. However, the name of the rune, Berkana, literally means "birch tree," or possibly "poplar," although it also has symbolic links with fir trees of all types. The rune's association with growing things also connects it with agriculture.

The feminine rune Berkana is associated with the graceful swan. The swan's proverbial protectiveness of its cygnets is an eloquent indication of Berkana's maternal nature.

Mother love and caring for infants are Berkana's main meanings. Other associations include marital fidelity and domestic harmony.

MYTHOLOGY

As might be imagined with such a feminine rune, its mythology derives from the stories of several Norse goddesses. Prominent among these is Frigga, the goddess of the spinning wheel and the wife of Odin, who has been previously encountered with the runes Wunjo (see page 46) and Pertho (page 66). Frigga was the patroness of women, especially those in labor or caring for infants, of marital fidelity, and family harmony. Fiercely protective of her own children, she nevertheless found time to care for the offspring of others, too. In one of her aspects, that of Brechta (literally meaning "birch"), she guarded the souls of young children. It is interesting to note that in past times, if a marriage ceremony was thought to be too expensive, the union could still be recognized if the prospective bride and groom jumped over a birch-twig broom together. The symbolism of the birch-twig broom leads us to the medieval traditions of witchcraft, because in old stories a witch and her broom were rarely parted. It may be that brooms did indeed play a role in a half-remembered matriarchal pagan cult that survived into recent history. This could be especially significant since women accused of being witches were often local healers and midwives.

UPRIGHT MEANING

Berkana is a rune of new beginnings. It indicates good news, birth, fertility, and times of family rejoicing, such as weddings. The rune's link with the birch tree in particular, and agriculture in general, shows that a time of personal growth is on the way. This may involve material, domestic, or – by far the most likely possibility – spiritual affairs, because Berkana is also associated with intuition, the higher self and the soul's purpose on earth. As a more specific indicator, Berkana suggests that a new project is getting off the ground, but will need rigorous care and attention if it is to thrive, much as a human infant needs the loving care of its mother in order to thrive and develop.

Traditionally, Berkana relates to women's issues, particularly to feminine health and the

care of infants. In its upright position, the rune can be regarded as a good omen that denotes proper growth and development. If your question is about a health problem, the appearance of Berkana symbolizes natural regenerative powers and a raising of the spirits as a sense of well-being returns.

INVERTED MEANING

Worrying family news is often indicated when Berkana is inverted. The health of a relative is the most usual reason for this anxiety. There is a hint that a celebration will be canceled or, at the very least, indefinitely postponed. If health is not the issue under examination, then the inverted Berkana indicates that you are on a course that will lead you nowhere. You will find that since all doors are closed to you at present, it will be necessary to cut your losses and return to square one.

Ehwaz

"Eoh is a joy to princes in the presence of warriors, a steed in the pride of its hooves, when rich men discuss it, it is ever a comfort to the restless."

"THE ANGLO-SAXON RUNE POEM"

ALTERNATIVE NAMES

The Anglo-Saxons of England knew this rune as Eoh.

PRONUNCIATION

"E."

KEY CONCEPTS

Ehwaz (not to be confused with Eihwaz in the second sequence) is said to represent a pair of horses at full gallop, their eight hooves pounding the ground. In modern terms, this has an obvious association with vehicles and travel in general. The "vehicle of the soul," or physical body, is also symbolized by it. Since Ehwaz represents a team of horses, relationships of all kinds fall under the auspices of this rune. Status, too, forms part of its symbolism, because in ancient times to own a fine horse was a mark of exalted rank, while to own a team took one into the realms of the higher aristocracy. It is also said that apart from horses, all other domesticated animals are symbolized by Ehwaz. In terms of plants, the rune relates to the apple tree and has associations with the oak and the ash. Its associated herb is the humble ragwort.

Pets and domestic livestock, as well as the aristocracy, are represented by the rune Ehwaz.

MYTHOLOGY

The most obvious mythological link with Ehwaz is Sleipnir, the steed of Odin, which was said to have eight legs reminiscent of the runic symbolism of eight hooves pounding the ground. However, there is a semi-legendary link to be found in early English history. The first Anglo-Saxons to come to England during the reign of King Vortigern were called Hengist and Horsa. These names mean "stallion" and "horse" respectively. To this day, the symbol of the English county of Kent, the landing place of Hengist and Horsa, is a white horse. This symbol is seen on a vast scale in Southern England as well, where the equine form has been cut into chalk hillsides. It is also interesting to note that England itself may take its name from a horse god named Ing, who was considered to be an aspect of the fertility god Frey (see Raido, page 37, and Inguz, page 92). It is therefore likely that when Hengist and Horsa landed on the shores of England, a land that was unknown to them, they bore a banner that was emblazoned with the rune Ehwaz.

Ehwaz is the third rune to be associated with horses and transport in general. A modern interpretation of this rune connects its symbolism with the automobile, the "horse" of modern times.

UPRIGHT MEANING

When Ehwaz appears either singly or as the first rune of a reading, you can be sure that things are picking up in pace and changing for the better. This is a rune of large concepts, of major projects, and new and exciting adventures. It is also said to emphasize the meanings of the other runes of the reading and to speed up the events that they foretell. The most usual interpretation of Ehwaz indicates travel, usually to a new location that will provide the physical and mental stimulation that you crave. However, it might equally indicate a move of home or the establishment of a partnership with a person who is as strong-willed as you are. The importance of forming a team, of running in harness, and not falling out of step, is suggested, too. It also denotes the need to treat your partners with the respect that they deserve, demonstrating

your loyalty, consulting them on important issues and ensuring that the bonds between you remain strong, despite the challenges that are in store. The rune may have a connection with higher education, especially if you are involved in subjects that are investigative, such as the sciences. However the Ehwaz rune manifests itself in your life, an increase in your personal status and that of those around you is certain.

INVERTED MEANING

Problems with traveling and vehicles are suggested when this rune is inverted. Your friends and family may not be in tune with your ideas, and this frustrates your ambition with unnecessary delays. There may also be health worries in connection with pets and domestic animals.

Mannaz

"Madr is the joy of mankind and an augmentation of dust and the adorner of ships."

"THE ICELANDIC RUNE POEM"

ALTERNATIVE NAMES

This rune was also known as Mann or Madr.

PRONUNCIATION

"M."

KEY CONCEPTS

Mannaz is the rune of humankind. Its variant name, Mann, should not be taken to mean that only those of the male gender are referred to, however. On the contrary, both men and women, all of the family of humankind, are in a sense governed by this rune. In runic tradition, one of the main traits of humanity is the faculty of foresight, thus the symbolism of Mannaz is enriched by its identification with the keen-eyed hawk. In terms of the vegetable kingdom, the rune is associated with the ash and the elm. This link is made because Norse mythology states that the very first humans were fashioned from the wood of the ash and elm trees.

Mannaz is the rune of humankind. Tacitus wrote that a god named Mannus was the ancestor of humanity, and families and lines of descent are associated with this rune.

MYTHOLOGY

Although any myth that relates to the doings of humankind can be said to be relevant to this rune, the acts of Heimdall, the "god who stands between," are notable. During one of his periods of wandering on the earth, Heimdall, in the guise of Rigr, stayed overnight with three different married couples. In each case he slept with his host's wife before moving on. In the fullness of time, three sons were born to these women. The first was named Thrall, the second was called Karl, and the third Jarl or Earl. These three men were regarded as being the ancestors of the three classes of Nordic society, Earl being the first of the nobles, Karl of the warriors, and Thrall the progenitor of the peasants. Thus Heimdall, or Rigr, became the ancestor of humankind and was the first god to pass on the knowledge of the runes to his mortal offspring. Furthering this story slightly, Jarl was said to have been the father of Konur, the first king of Denmark.

The keen-eyed hawk is symbolic of the ever-vigilant Heimdall, who, in his incarnation as Rigr, was another god who was credited with being the ancestor of humankind.

UPRIGHT MEANING

The appearance of Mannaz always relates directly to the person who has asked the question. It may signify your status and the way that others tend to perceive you. It also serves as a reminder that we are all products of our experiences and urges you to take a good look at your own conduct before criticizing those around you. The rune may well have further implications: it can reveal that you have been deluding yourself and that you are not the person that you thought yourself to be. So when this rune is prominent in your reading, it is time for a reassessment and an examination of your motives and aims. Equally, the motives of others should come under scrutiny, and you should ask some searching questions before committing yourself to anything binding. Mannaz is not a rune of haste, so if important decisions are to be made and Mannaz

appears in a reading, take your time, consult a trusted advisor who has no personal interest in the situation and wait to see what develops. Legal affairs and far-reaching decisions are likely when this rune is drawn, but this is no reason to panic. If you slow down and look within yourself, it is likely that you will find the right solution.

INVERTED MEANING

When this rune is inverted, you must be aware that someone close to you bears you ill will. In a negative position, Mannaz usually indicates an enemy, but this is not always so. For instance, some rune readers suggest that it can denote male homosexuality or the nervousness and lack of courage that is the result of a life blighted by an overly strict father or other harsh authority figure. Look to the next rune in your reading for advice.

Laguz

"Logr is the welling stream and broad geyser and the land of fish."

"THE ICELANDIC RUNE POEM"

ALTERNATIVE NAMES

The Anglo-Saxons knew this rune as Lagu, while the more northerly Germanic peoples called it Logr.

PRONUNCIATION

"L."

KEY CONCEPTS

As the words of the rune poem above imply, Laguz is a rune of water. It is closely connected with the tides, both those that occur in the sea and those that are found in the human heart. The shape of the upright rune is said to denote a swelling tide, while its inverted form represents the ebb. The symbols of Laguz are almost exclusively of the sea, or at least semi-aquatic in nature. In the animal kingdom, the otter and the seal are prominent. Its birds are the gull and the cormorant. Even its symbolic tree, the willow, is often found on the banks of lakes, pools, and streams. Of course, the sleek ships of the Vikings fell under its auspices as, indeed, do sea shells.

All of the symbols of the rune laguz either pertain to the sea or are aquatic in nature. The swift-flowing stream and placid lake are equally potent representations of this, the most watery of runes.

MYTHOLOGY

Although the seafaring races of the north worshiped some fearsome divinities who dwelled in the depths, they also looked to a more kindly god called Njord to lend them a helping hand. Njord was one of the elemental Vanir gods and the father of Frey and Freya. Although he and his wife (or sister), Nerthus, are rather obscure figures that lack the wild glamor of such gods as Thor and Odin, they were credited with providing sustenance from the sea and also from the earth. Nerthus was more concerned with the abundance of crops, while Njord provided good fishing and fair weather for sailing. Because Njord was also married to Skadi, the goddess who lent her name to Scandinavia, this gentle sea god can also be regarded as the deity of fjords, safe inlets, and harbors.

Njord, the benign sea god, was the patron of every good thing that the sea produces for the benefit of humankind and also ensured productive fishing and fair sailing. The seashell was his personal symbol.

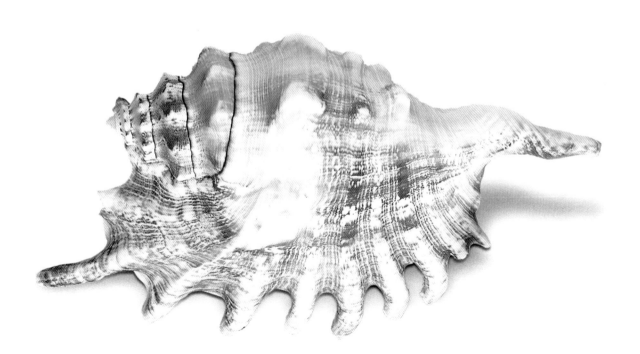

UPRIGHT MEANING

Laguz is a rune that signifies deep spiritual love. It is a particularly good omen to receive as an answer to a relationship question. Even if your love life is going through some stormy times, this rune indicates that you will come through the upheavals of the waves of emotion and will find a safe haven once more. Laguz can also be regarded as a rune of travel, especially over the sea. Inner journeys are signified by Laguz, too, which symbolizes the depths of the soul. It may furthermore have indications of fertility because it is one of the runes favorable to pregnancy. In more material concerns, too, Laguz promises material good fortune and success. It should be remembered that the ancient Norse peoples were traders, as well as pirates, and to them the sea was a trackless path to wealth. However, as in the sea, there is an ebb and flow in the tides of life, and you may have to wait a while before things move in your

direction. Remember that anything worth having is worth waiting for, and that all you need to do is to have patience for good fortune to flow to you. You may be feeling somewhat powerless when the Laguz rune is drawn: other people may seem to be making all the moves and you can only wait for your turn. Remember that this is a rune of good fortune and that your turn will surely come. There is an old prayer that asks for God to send a fair wind. Send it he will, but you will have to hoist your own sails to make the most of it.

INVERTED MEANING

When inverted, this rune is overly emotional and disturbing. If you draw Laguz in the inverted position, it could denote that you are being too assertive. Demanding immediate results in an aggressive manner is counterproductive. You may be cursing fate for some misfortune and drowning your sorrows with alcohol. Try to be more logical. Exercise patience a little more and, above all, be calm.

Inguz

"Ing was amongst the East-Danes first seen by men, till later he went over the wave; his wain followed after; the Headings named the hero so."

"THE ANGLO-SAXON RUNE POEM"

ALTERNATIVE NAMES

This rune had no Scandinavian equivalent, although the Anglo-Saxons often contracted its name to Ing, which is also the name of the horse god of fertility.

PRONUNCIATION

"NG," as in "thing."

KEY CONCEPTS

Although Ing-Frey was a horse god, the main symbolic associations of this rune deals with another totem beast of his, the boar. The cuckoo is its bird symbol, while laurels and apple trees, and the herbs rosemary and self-heal, are its vegetational correspondents. The shape of the rune suggests a doorway, and many rune masters consider Inguz to be a portal to the astral plane. In Germanic languages, names that end in the "ing" sound denote "son of" (the Saxon heir to the throne being called the "atheling" or "son of the king").

Inguz is thought to represent a doorway, not only in the sense of an ordinary entrance, but also a mystical portal between the worlds.

The popular deity Frey, the god of the fertility of the earth, rode a boar whose golden bristles symbolize a field of ripening wheat.

MYTHOLOGY

Frey, the Norse god of the earth's fertility, is the primary deity associated with the rune Inguz. He is also identified – although tenuously – as the god of horses, Ing or Ing-Frey. However, Frey did not actually ride a horse. His preferred steed was a wild boar named Gullinbursti, or "golden bristles." The bristles on the boar's back symbolized fields of ripening wheat. Although most sources refer to Ing and Frey as being one and the same, there is an element of doubt regarding this identification. As the "ing" sound often denotes "son of," Ing-Frey may not have been Frey himself, but rather his unnamed son. He also appears to have been a semihistorical person who, in words of the rune poem on page 91, "was amongst the East-Danes first seen by men."

MEANING

Inguz is particularly concerned with the health, fertility, and well-being of men. It often denotes fertility of mind, or the motivation and energy needed to start new projects. A new job is often indicated when this rune is drawn, but even if this does not occur, the potential remains for considerable change for the better. Of course, for a new phase in life to begin, it is necessary to finish old business and turn away from situations that are leading nowhere. Don't worry that nothing will come to replace them: new and more productive opportunities will arrive. Inguz is also a rune of problem-solving, so if a complex matter has taken up your time and attention, its solution is not far away. Ignoring the problem for a while might help, because you may be so involved in its intricacies that you cannot see the bigger picture. When you return with fresh insight, the solution will be obvious. It may also be time that you took a vacation. Inguz often denotes that you should put your house in order, clear away any rubbish, and focus your attention on the harmony of your  surroundings. The implications of the rune go farther: perhaps certain people are sapping your confidence and taking advantage of your good will. If so, these folk should no longer play a role in your life. You will need courage, foresight, and wisdom to detect who, and what, you need around you and what is redundant. Inguz may also have a bearing on inheritance, both the passing on of material goods through the generations and the continuance of the traditions and traits of forebears.

The appearance of Inguz is often an indication that one should put one's house in order. In order to make progress, cluttered surroundings and confused thinking must be cleared and clarified.

Othila

"Epel is dear to all men, if they may enjoy there at home whatever is right and proper in continual prosperity."

"THE ANGLO-SAXON RUNE POEM"

ALTERNATIVE NAMES

The Anglo Saxons knew this rune as either Epel or Ethel.

PRONUNCIATION

"O."

KEY CONCEPTS

The oldest literal meaning of this rune is "nobility" or "prince." Othila is related to the first syllable of the Saxon word "atheling," meaning "heir to the throne" (see Inguz, page 91). The modern German word *adel* and the Dutch *edel* are both derived from Othila, and both of these words have connotations with aristocracy. The rune therefore points to the rightful claim to inherited status, lands, and possessions. It also indicates *noblesse oblige*, the obligations of one's position in society and the duties that one owes to one's kin and people. Of course, there is also the added implication of loyalty that the people owe to their monarch. Othila is symbolized by the

Othila is symbolically associated with royalty and rulers. The literal meaning of the word is "nobility" or "prince."

hawthorn tree and the humble clover, but its most important symbolic association is with Odin, the king of the gods of Asgard.

MYTHOLOGY

This rune provides the initial letter of Odin's name and is considered especially sacred to him. Although Othila denotes nobility, and even kingship, it is also a rune of sacrifice. After all, what modern monarch or head of state could possibly lead a normal life? The very position implies the sacrifice of personal freedom, and in many cases throughout history it has been necessary for such leaders eventually to sacrifice their lives as well. So it was with Odin, who hung himself upon the windy tree to win the knowledge of the runes for the good of all, gods and humankind alike. Until recent times, a king was thought of as representing the luck of his subjects: if he thrived, then so did the land; if he ailed, it was believed that his land and people would suffer. At least modern monarchs do not have to worry about being sacrificed if their powers wane, as was the case in ancient Europe.

Because of the Othila rune's associations with godhood, it is symbolically linked with the clover, the leaves of which were used by St. Patrick of Ireland to explain the mystery of the Holy Trinity.

UPRIGHT MEANING

Othila represents a time when hallowed traditions will become increasingly important. The rune suggests something that stands the test of time, a set of values that is fixed, immovable, and strangely comforting. In addition, the true meaning of loyalty is the most common interpretation of Othila. This loyalty can be expressed in any number of ways: patriotism, devotion to a particular religion, or identification with a group whose aims you share. However, group loyalty is most common in those who share a heritage, namely a family. The rune may signify a rightful inheritance, but this need not necessarily mean a bequest of property or money, although they may not be unlikely. It could denote traits that have come down through the generations that express a certain correctness of behavior and a sense of belonging. Justice and honor are also associated with the appearance of this rune. Because of the dynastic implications of Othila, engagements and marriages can be denoted. Issues involving children, our eventual heirs, will turn out favorably. You may find yourself dealing with wills and property and may need advice from older and wiser heads to chart a course through the paperwork. An advantageous move of home could be indicated, too, especially so if it somehow brings you closer to your origins.

INVERTED MEANING

Disloyalty and the overturning of established principles are likely when this rune is found in the inverted position. Disputes over inheritance and quarrels about money and status are equally likely when Othila is inverted. A loss of some kind is shown, possibly due to theft or legal chicanery. Modern interpreters often suggest that an inverted Othila predicts accidents and problems with machinery.

Dagaz

"Daeg, the glorious light of the Sun is sent by the High One, is beloved of men, a source of hope and happiness to rich and poor alike, of service to all."

"THE ANGLO-SAXON RUNE POEM"

ALTERNATIVE NAMES

The Anglo-Saxon name for this rune, Daeg, is related to the word for "day" in many European languages.

PRONUNCIATION

"D."

KEY CONCEPTS

Dagaz represents noon, when the Sun is at the highest point of its course. It also means daylight itself, especially the long hours of glorious sunshine at midsummer, which are the primary symbolic elements of this rune. If the twenty-four runes are laid out in a circle, then Dagaz will appear at precisely the opposite point to Jera. In the runic calendar, Jera represents midwinter, when the Sun is at its weakest, and Dagaz symbolizes the Sun in its full strength. The rowan tree and Norway spruce are the trees associated with Dagaz. It is also symbolized by the herb sage.

Dagaz is associated with midday and represents the glorious light of the Sun at its maximum strength. In an extension of this concept, the rune also symbolizes the summer solstice.

MYTHOLOGY

Because Dagaz is elementally governed by fire, two fire gods of radically differing characteristics are associated with it. The first is Heimdall, symbolized by a steady torch or beacon shining in the darkness. Heimdall was the sentinel of the gods, the guardian of the rainbow bridge, ever watchful and the bringer of enlightenment to mortals (it was he who revealed the secrets of the runes to humankind, see Kaunaz, page 40, and Mannaz, page 86). The other god connected with Dagaz is the untrustworthy Loki, the trickster. Loki was too clever for his own, or, indeed, anyone else's, good. Although he did some beneficial things, these boons were usually a by-product of his mischievous acts. Even so, he was the blood brother of Odin and was usually cunning enough to talk his way out of trouble. Loki represents wild, uncontrolled flames, and is an enemy of humans, while Heimdall represents warmth, security, and illumination. The two gods were great rivals and were fated to kill each other on the dreadful day of Ragnarok.

In contrast to the kindly light of Heimdall, the cunning Loki represents the flames of an uncontrollable wild fire. This god's wicked sense of humor made him an enemy of humankind.

MEANING

Dagaz is a rune of happiness and prosperity. It does, however, suggest that major changes will soon occur. Yet this rune is also one of laughter, fun, and wonderful new experiences. Dagaz is a good rune to receive if you have been suspended in a period of waiting as it signifies the end of an era and the beginning of a new one. A fresh burst of activity is to be expected when this rune appears. It can also show a breakthrough following a period of frustration that exposes previously hidden information. Indeed, secrets are about to be revealed when Dagaz makes an appearance. It will motivate your actions and lead you to a position from which you can take an enlightened stance on any issue that troubles you. This new enlightenment will give you the

opportunity to plan for the future sensibly. However, Dagaz is not all about serious life-path changes and there is a strong element of fun in the rune. In some cases, it signals playtime because the new perspective that it gives reveals that life isn't all hard work and self-denial. You may find new avenues to explore with childlike wonder. A marvelous sense of humor is evident, too, proving that life is worth living. This association with childhood goes beyond you personally. In fact, anything to do with children is auspicious. Most rune readers think that Dagaz is always beneficial, having no inverted meaning. However, should this rune appear in a negative position or fall face down repeatedly, it signals the end of an era and warns that you may have to wait a while before the new beginning occurs.

Dagaz is the rune of new experiences, and of childlike wondering at the marvelous things found in the world. It also denotes good fortune for children generally.

Wyrd: the blank rune

Many modern rune readers have introduced an extra, blank rune to the accepted symbols of the Elder Futhark. However, since the runes are essentially an alphabet, and each rune represents a letter, there is very little justification for this. After all, each letter signifies a sound, or combination of sounds, and even in the modern alphabet there is no symbol that represents silence. In addition, there is no historical evidence whatsoever that the rune masters of the past ever included a blank

stone or stick either in their divinations or in the runic calendar.

Some modern practitioners of runic divination have given the blank rune the name Wyrd, a word that literally means "fate." The Norns were said to weave the web of Wyrd, in other words, creating the destiny to which we are all individually bound. In turn, according to some myths, the Norns were the daughters of a mysterious goddess called Wyrd, who seems to be little more than a personification

Wyrd, the blank rune, can be interpreted as the workings of fate, symbolized by the unpredictable fall of the dice.

of their collective function. One interpretation of the blank rune is that it signals that fate has taken a hand in your affairs and that you should look no farther into the reading. However, this is a function that is already present in the Elder Futhark, found under Pertho (see page 67). The function of fate as a necessity can likewise be found within the meaning of the rune Nauthiz (see page 53). In summary, the Wyrd rune does not belong to any of the three aetts of the Elder Futhark.

For those who wish to use the blank rune in their readings, however, here are a few suggestions as to its possible interpretation. The Anglo-Saxons and other races of Northern Europe believed in a universal force that they called Orlog. Orlog, which literally means "doom" or "destiny," governed the fate of nations and entire populations (in fact, there is a Dutch word, *oorlog*, which means "war"). In terms of this rune, Orlog should be taken to mean the individual fate that is our birthright. It expresses the karmic debt, which many believe has been carried over from a previous life. According to this view, most of the important elements of life are already predestined and nothing can be done to change them. When the blank rune turns up, it means that you are reaching such a point and that there is absolutely nothing you can do to change it. Although free will exists, at this moment events will go as they have been ordained.

Although some interpreters believe that the blank rune is indicative of grief and despair, this narrow view misunderstands the complexities of Wyrd.

If the blank rune turns up as the answer to a specific question, the answer is that this is not the right time to ask it.

The blank rune also indicates major changes in your life. Some even suggest that a bereavement is likely. However, since the rune has no symbolic associations, it would be difficult to work out if this is the case.

In my opinion, the use of Wyrd, the blank rune, is not necessary to runic divination, and is simply a modern addition to the ancient practice of rune-casting.

THE ART OF
reading runes

The runes of the Elder Futhark can be read in many ways. Many people prefer to draw a single rune to provide a complete reading in itself. Others literally cast the runes onto a plain, white cloth and allow their intuition to guide them. There is also a more formal technique in which the runes are arranged in various meaningful patterns (these arrangements are correctly known as "shoats"). A selection of these patterns will be dealt with under rune-casting, pages 105–17.

The runes must be thoroughly mixed before any reading can commence.

One method of mixing the runes is to shake them in a bag and then to select a number of them at random.

How to begin

It doesn't really matter whether you are reading the runes for yourself or for someone else, because the mental process for the rune reader remains the same in either case. Take a few deep breaths to help you to calm your system and clear any extraneous thoughts from your mind. Allow yourself to drift into a passive mental state as you play with the runes to mix them. If you keep your runes in a bag, then at this point you should be shaking the bag to make sure that they are randomly jumbled together. If you use rune staves (see the method of Tacitus, page105,) then you can simply hold them in your hand at this point.

When you are content that you are in a receptive frame of mind and that the runes are well mixed, you may then either cast them or pick some out and lay them in one of the set patterns. If you are rune-reading for someone else, he or she will have to mix the runes together thoroughly before you do this. If you have, or the person you are reading for has, a specific question, this query should be thought about while the runes are being mixed. It may be helpful to ask this question out loud just as the runes are laid down, but this is not strictly necessary if privacy is an issue.

Reading the runes for yourself

No matter how you choose to consult the runes, it is important to bear in mind that their meaning may not be immediately obvious to you. One cannot help but be subjective about one's own life, so you are bound to have strong preconceptions about what the runes will reveal, even before the first one is cast. You may be presented with the answer to a pressing question, only to find that you don't understand it. Having said that, it is possible to read the runes for yourself. One way of getting around the difficulties involved is to keep a rune notebook and write down the names, meanings, and positions of the runes for future reference. You will find that it is easier to interpret their often subtle message once you have taken a step back, so to speak, and can look at them again with a cool head.

The actual process of reading a rune-casting is set out on page 102. Simply adapt the first to fourth steps so that they relate to yourself.

The runes can provide valuable clues as to the workings of fate and give a glimpse into the future.

Reading the runes for others

The most important thing to bear in mind when reading the runes is that these mysterious, ancient symbols are never, ever flippant. Even if they are consulted on a trivial matter, the runes will swiftly strip away the nonsense and address an issue that is much more important and life-changing. Like Tarot cards and other forms of divination, the runes will tend to focus on dramatic events, strong emotions and periods of soul-searching. If you draw a single rune to provide the reading, it is important to remember that this drama may either have occurred in the past, be happening right now, or will manifest itself in the future. Whatever it might be, you can be sure that the runes will home in on it so, don't immediately assume that a troubling rune, such as Hagalaz or Uruz, is the certain next step in a person's fate. The event indicated might just as easily have already happened and it may be that you are being consulted in the aftermath of the experience.

THE FIRST STEP

When you begin a rune reading, it is a good idea not to attempt to look into the future immediately. Begin by drawing a single rune to represent the background to the reading. It may be that this rune alone will immediately answer the unspoken question of your client and provide the solution to a problem. However, it may just as easily reveal the problem that is weighing on your client's mind.

THE SECOND STEP

After interpreting this initial rune, put it back with the others and turn your attention to the present circumstances. You may choose either to draw another single rune to represent the present or to lay out a few runes in one of the simple arrangements, such as the three Norns pattern (page 107), to provide a general impression of the present circumstances. If this portion of the reading is accurate, you can safely assume that your attempt to part the veil of the future will be too. Now return the runes to their bag or pile and mix them again.

It is possible to translate names or initials into runic equivalents. This method can provide additional insights into character and fate.

THE THIRD STEP

The person for whom you are reading should now mix the runes together and choose a number of runes to represent the general pattern of the future. It's best if you have already decided which arrangement is to be used and can tell the enquirer how many runes are needed. If you like, you can literally cast all of the runes onto a plain, flat surface (tradition suggests a plain, white cloth) and allow your intuition to guide you to the ones that are to be read. However, this is generally considered to be too confusing for a beginner, so perhaps at this stage it's best if you stick to one of the more formal arrangements.

THE FOURTH STEP

If the person for whom you are reading does not feel that their concerns have been adequately dealt with by now, you can return to the first or second step to answer any specific questions. Remember, the runes never provide flippant answers, so if they start to repeat the messages that they have already given, that is all that your client is permitted to know at this time. You may also wish to examine your client's date and time of birth according to the runic calendar (pages 118–22) to ascertain their life purpose. It might also be an idea to translate your client's initials into runic script (pages 123–25) to provide further information concerning their character and fate.

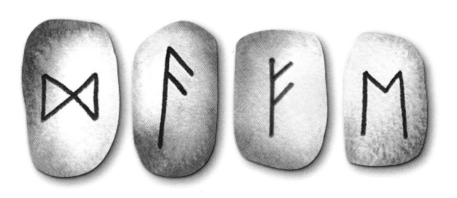

Rune-casting

1. THE METHOD OF TACITUS

The ancient Roman author Tacitus wrote of a method of divination that was in general use amongst the Teutonic peoples of his time (see page 11). A similar method employed today involves cutting nine straight, short twigs, preferably from a fruit-bearing tree. Having said that, nine matches or lollipop sticks will usually do just as well. These sticks are called rune staves.

The first step in performing a divination with the rune staves is to lay down a white cloth. You then hold the staves in your hand while allowing your mind to drift into a passive state. Think about the question that you wish to ask the runes. When you are ready, cast the staves onto the cloth.

Take a moment to examine the shapes that the jumbled sticks make. If you see an obviously runic shape among the sticks, then make a note of it. This will be the first rune of your reading.

Gather the staves together once more and repeat the process, making a note of any runic symbol that occurs. Repeat the entire process for a third time. You should now have sufficient runes to provide a complete reading.

It may be that you cannot immediately make out the rune shapes in the jumble of staves. Conversely, you could detect more than one rune per casting. In this case, make

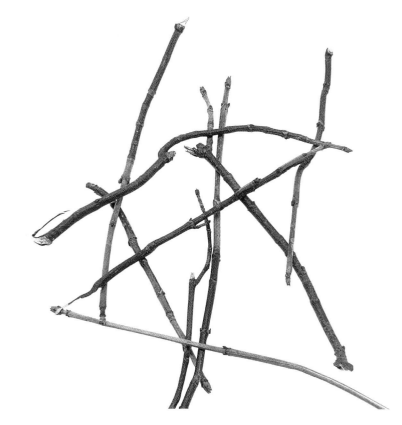

First cast nine rune staves at random.

Here you can see Rune Gebo

Here you can see Rune Kaunaz

Here you can see Rune Wunjo

a note of them all in the order that you noticed them. These runes will provide the answers to your question. You may also find that the three casts of the staves only provide you with a single rune. If this happens, don't worry: that rune will indeed give the answer to your query.

EXAMPLE: Using three castings of the rune staves, the following three runes were revealed: Kaunaz, Hagalaz, and, finally, Wunjo. These can now be read in the order of past, present, and future. This suggests that the enquirer has learned a great deal in the past and has gained remarkable insight (Kaunaz). The present, however, seems to be fraught with anxiety and a period of bad luck has befallen the enquirer (Hagalaz). The future, though, looks much brighter as a result of the appearance of Wunjo, the rune of happy-ever-afters. There may also be a new love affair in the offing.

2. ODIN'S RUNE

This type of divination is the simplest of all runic readings. It involves quietening the mind, allowing a passive mental state to occur, and then choosing one rune to answer a specific question, or, if used daily, to provide a subject for meditation. You could also choose a rune before going to bed to reveal what the events of the day meant. However, there are considerations to be aware of when using this method: remember that the runes are never flippant and that a single rune may highlight a particular issue without revealing either the answer to a question or the outcome. If you are a novice rune reader, then I would recommend using Odin's rune method as the background to a more general reading rather than as a reading in itself.

EXAMPLE: The rune drawn was Tiwaz, showing that a firm conviction that the enquirer is doing the right thing, acting with honorable intentions, and being ready to play fair in all dealings is the only sure way to win success. Legal decisions will also tend to favor the enquirer (see Tiwaz, page 76).

3. THE THREE NORNS METHOD

This method is named after the three goddesses of fate and involves drawing three runes in precisely the same way as for the single-rune method. The three are then placed side by side and read in the order that they were drawn. As the casting's name implies, this method gives a specific reading relating to the past, present, and future. The runes of the three Norns method are traditionally read from right to left.

Position 1. The Place of Urd
A rune in this position reveals events in the past that have direct relevance to the present situation and form the foundations of the future.

Position 2. The Place of Verdandi
This rune refers to present circumstances and will point out any choices that will have to be made in the very near future.

Position 3. The Place of Skuld
This is likely to be the most difficult rune to interpret because it relates to the veiled future. It may reveal an aspect of your fate that is as yet unknown. It may equally either show the outcome of current trends or provide a possible future scenario that is dependent on the choices that you make.

Hold the runes in your hand while allowing a question to form in your mind. When you feel that you are ready, cast the runes..

4. THE NINE-RUNE CAST

This is a method that is very close to the classical rune-casting written about by Tacitus. Although there is no formal arrangement of the runes in this method, it is nevertheless a very revealing way of consulting the mysteries of fate. Although your intuition is the most important factor when consulting the runes in this way, there are certain rules that will help you to make sense of the fall of the runes. The best way to do this is to make a note of each rune in turn and possibly also to sketch their relative positions in your notebook.

STEP 1

Randomly pick nine runes from your pile. Hold them in your hands while allowing a question to form in your mind. When you consider yourself to be in a receptive mental state, cast the nine runes onto a white cloth. You will find that a number will land face upward, while others will be inverted. Those that are upright should be read first (remember to make a note of them in your rune notebook). These runes will reveal the situation that you find yourself in, as well as showing the factors in the past that have led to it.

A scattering of nine runes on a white cloth.

STEP 2

Once you have done this, look at the runes that lie at the center of the cloth. Runes in the center are very important, and you should take your time interpreting them. They may advise you on what decisions to make, warn you of future pitfalls, or reveal hitherto unknown influences coming into your life.

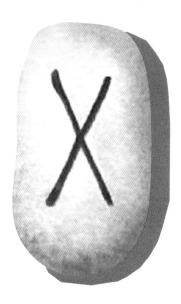

STEP 3

Now look at the runes that are lying face up on the edges of the cloth (if some have left the cloth entirely, their importance is diminished to the point at which they can be ignored). The general rule is that the farther a rune is from the center, the less important it will be. These runes will show the influence of others on your question.

STEP 4

Now look at the runes that have landed face down. These represent the future and should be read in the order that you turn them over, ensuring that they remain in the same position relative to the other runes. You will find that another level of reading is now possible because the individual runes will form group-ings. Some will be found in pairs, others singly, or in threes. You can then apply the rules of the single-rune and three Norns methods to find out more about the hidden meanings of the runic symbols.

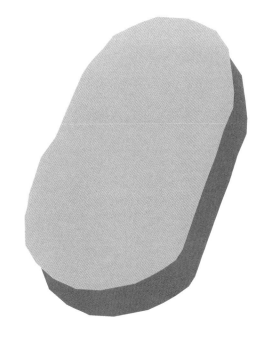

The Lo Shu magic square with numbers.

5. THE SQUARE OF NINE

This arrangement of rune stones is an elaboration of the three Norns method and deals with the past, present, and future. However, it also takes into account people and events that you may not be aware of and their bearing on the matter in hand. This reading also reveals your desires and unconscious attitudes. This method is particularly interesting because it involves the use of the "magic square." This pattern is a 3x3 grid that in other European and Middle Eastern forms of mysticism is called the "square of Saturn." It also turns up in the traditions of the Orient, while the pattern additionally forms the basis of "Compass School" Feng Shui.

Runes set out in accordance with the square of nine method

4	9	2
3	5	7
8	1	6

As with the nine-rune cast, choose nine runes at random from your pile. These should then be laid out in order, according to the positions given in the above diagram.

POSITION 1. The past and its bearing on present events.

POSITION 2. Your future state of mind and attitude to the outcome.

POSITION 3. Influences on the matter in hand that you may not be aware of.

POSITION 4. How these hidden influences will affect the outcome.

POSITION 5. Present circumstances.

POSITION 6. Your memories of, and attitude to, past events.

POSITION 7. Your present viewpoint.

POSITION 8. Hidden influences on past events.

POSITION 9. The best possible outcome.

6. THE RUNIC CROSS

The runic cross uses six runes picked at random from your bag or pile. These are then laid out in the form of a single vertical made up of four runes, with a rune on either side of the main axis. The first rune is laid on the left, the second rune is second from bottom. The third is on the right, the fourth is placed at the base of the central column. The fifth rune is second from the top and, finally, the sixth is placed at the top of the cross.

The runic cross

POSITION 1
The past.

POSITION 2
The present.

POSITION 3
How you envisage the future.

POSITION 4
The background and reasons for the matter in hand.

POSITION 5
Obstacles and possible problems.

POSITION 6
The eventual outcome.

7. THE FIVE DIRECTIONS

This simple runic arrangement utilizes five randomly chosen runes. This is another pattern that is laid out in a crosslike formation. Start at the bottom of the cross shape. The second rune goes on the left and the third at the top. The fourth rune is placed on the right and, finally, the fifth in the center. This type of reading is suitable for answering a specific question. All of the runes should be placed face down and turned over one by one until the reading is completed.

POSITION 1
The past and its influence on the query.

POSITION 2
Problems and potential obstacles in your path.

POSITION 3
Strokes of luck and other beneficial influences working in your favor.

POSITION 4
The immediate outcome.

POSITION 5
This rune represents both the eventual outcome and the lesson that you should have learned from the experience.

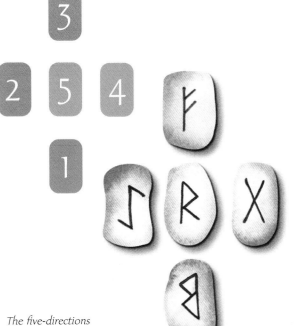

The five-directions arrangement.

Seven runes arranged in a "V" shape.

8 THE RUNIC V

As its name suggests, this pattern is made up of seven randomly chosen runes in the shape of the letter "V." The runes should be placed starting at the top of the left-hand arm of the "V." Place three runes in a downward-tending diagonal, one at the bottom (this is called the keystone) and then three more rising diagonally from it, tending toward the right. This shape is considered significant because it represents the sacred enclosures used by the priests of the ancient Norse in Scandinavia. This arrangement can be used for general readings or in answer to a specific question.

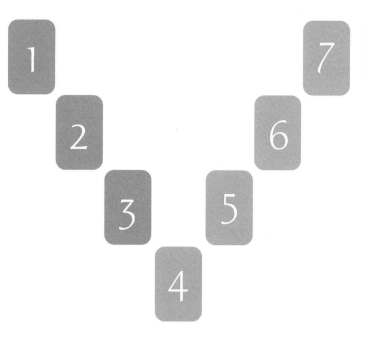

POSITION 1
The general influences of the past.

POSITION 2
Present circumstances.

POSITION 3
General prospects and hopes for the future.

POSITION 4
The keystone.
This is the most important rune in the reading. Take special note of it because it denotes the best possible course of action that you could take.

POSITION 5
The attitudes and emotional states of those around you.

POSITION 6
Potential problems that may delay or frustrate your plans.

POSITION 7
The outcome.

9. THE TIWAZ METHOD

This is the only rune arrangement that mimics the shape of an individual rune. The Tiwaz method is more complex than most of the others because it involves several stages before one ends up with a pattern that looks like the rune Tiwaz. Nevertheless, it is claimed that this arrangement is well worth the effort because, like Tiwaz itself, it never fails to be accurate.

STEP 1. Randomly choose four runes and arrange them in the form of a cross, similar to the five-directions method, but without the central stone. The runes should be laid in an anticlockwise direction, starting on the left. You may now read these runes according to the rules of the five-directions method (minus the final-outcome rune).

STEP 2. Now choose a further three runes. These may be read in accordance with the rules of the three Norns method. Once you have done this, place them in order around the original four runes in a clockwise manner, starting on the right. The placement of the first rune is diagonally down and slightly to the right of the cross shape that you already have. The second rune is below the cross shape and the final rune is diagonally to the left of the original pattern. You should end up with a pattern that looks like an upright arrowhead.

STEP 3. You can now begin to read the third stage of this divination, beginning with the rune on the far left and continuing as given on page 114.

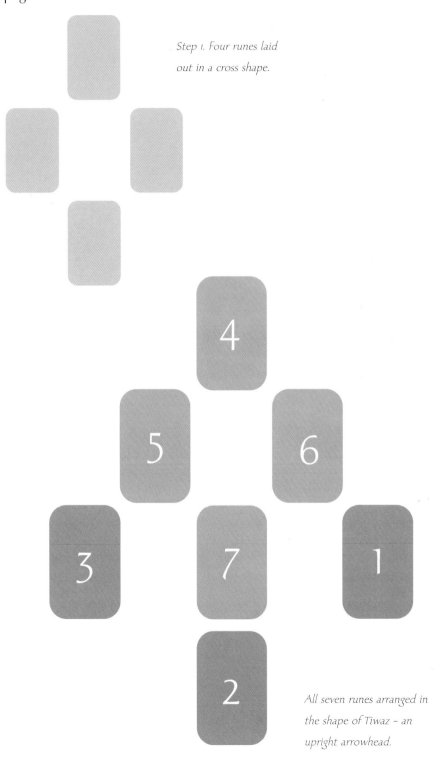

Step 1. Four runes laid out in a cross shape.

All seven runes arranged in the shape of Tiwaz – an upright arrowhead.

*The final arrangement of
the Tiwaz method should
resemble the shape of the
Tiwaz rune itself: an
upward-pointing
arrowhead.*

POSITION 4
Ill-advised actions that
may thwart your desires.

POSITION 5
Lessons learned in
the past from which you
may benefit.

POSITION 6
Your present position
and attitudes.

POSITION 1
The reasons for the
question and deep
feelings concerning it.

POSITION 3
Potential problems
confronting you.

POSITION 7
The outcome, for good
or ill.

POSITION 2
The best possible
outcome that can be
attained from present
circumstances.

10. THE WORLD TREE

The world-tree arrangement is another complex rune divination that comprises eleven randomly chosen runes. It is an elaboration on the square-of-nine method, with the addition of two extra runes to provide links between the three levels (although the order of the runes is different). This pattern makes up three levels: the lowest, called Utgard, refers to the past; the middle, called Midgard, refers to day-to-day life; and the upper, called Asgard, relates to spiritual life and the future. This is a particularly useful type of reading for questions of a spiritual nature.

The arrangement looks like a central axis comprising five runes, with three runes on either side of it. The first position is at the base of the vertical axis.

Numbered positions of the world-tree arrangement.

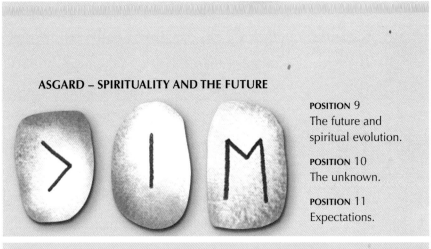

ASGARD – SPIRITUALITY AND THE FUTURE

POSITION 9
The future and spiritual evolution.

POSITION 10
The unknown.

POSITION 11
Expectations.

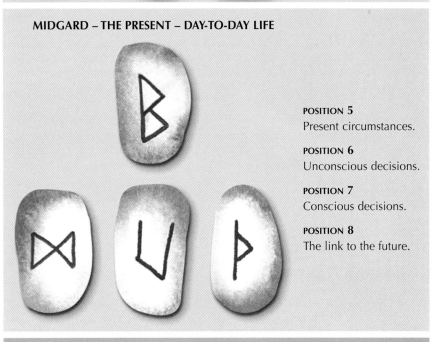

MIDGARD – THE PRESENT – DAY-TO-DAY LIFE

POSITION 5
Present circumstances.

POSITION 6
Unconscious decisions.

POSITION 7
Conscious decisions.

POSITION 8
The link to the future.

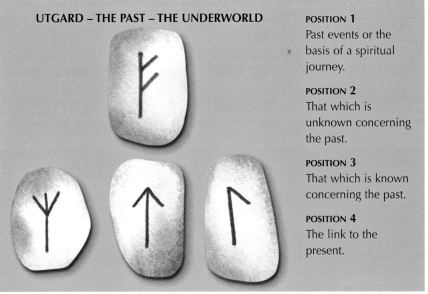

UTGARD – THE PAST – THE UNDERWORLD

POSITION 1
Past events or the basis of a spiritual journey.

POSITION 2
That which is unknown concerning the past.

POSITION 3
That which is known concerning the past.

POSITION 4
The link to the present.

11. THE RUNIC WHEEL

This is a type of reading based on the runic calendar (pages 118–22) and the eight directions of the compass. Eight randomly chosen runes are laid out in a circle in a clockwise direction, beginning in the east (in practice, this is the right-hand side of the arrangement). Each of the eight points of the wheel is named after a significant rune that represents not only a direction, but also a time period within the yearly cycle. For instance, the east is said to be the place of Berkana, relating to motherhood, children, fertility, and beginnings. The southeast is the place of Laguz, relating to water, safe havens, and abundance. Dagaz, Thurisaz, Kaunaz, Hagalaz, Jera, and Algiz follow in that order.

These particular runes are chosen to represent the points on the wheel because they also relate to significant periods in the ancient runic calendar. Berkana is symbolic of the spring equinox; Laguz represents the period around May Day; Dagaz symbolizes midsummer; and Thurisaz the festival of Lammas at the beginning of August. Kaunaz makes its appearance at the autumn equinox and is followed by Hagalaz at Hallowe'en; Jera represents Yuletide, the Christmas period, and, finally, Algiz symbolizes another ancient celebration, that of Candlemas, or the Feast of Purification, in early February.

At this point it important to bear in mind that these runes are only used as symbolic markers along the circumference of the runic wheel. You should randomize and choose eight runes in the usual manner. These will be laid out working in a clockwise direction, the first being placed on the right of the reading in the place of Berkana, the second in the place of Laguz, and so on. Supposing the first rune you chose was Fehu, this would be termed "Fehu in the place of Berkana." If you then chose Uruz, this would be "Uruz in the place of Laguz"; the third might be Thurisaz, in which case it would be described as "Thurisaz in the place of Dagaz." Should any rune you have chosen be the same as its corresponding place, such as Kaunaz in the place of Kaunaz, then this automatically makes it the single most important rune in the reading.

The runes of the runic wheel .

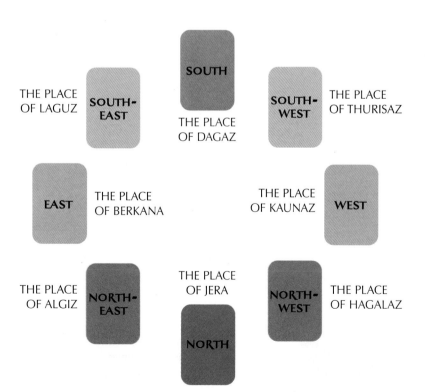

When reading the runic wheel, you may wish to consider the combination of the rune you have drawn and the place that it occupies, as well as examining the relationships of the runes themselves. This arrangement can also be useful in timing your reading and pinning down events to the relevant time of the year.

SOUTH
The place of Dagaz
(noon, heat, light,
warmth, sudden change).

SOUTH-EAST
The place of Laguz
(water, travel,
abundance and safe
havens)

SOUTH-WEST
The place of Thurisaz
(power, force and
protection from danger).

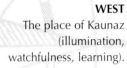

EAST
The place of Berkana
(motherhood, fertility,
births, beginnings).

WEST
The place of Kaunaz
(illumination,
watchfulness, learning).

NORTH
The place of Jera
(completion, celebration,
success).

NORTH-EAST
The place of Algiz
(inner strength, the
outcome).

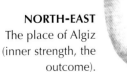

NORTH-WEST
The place of Hagalaz
(harsh realities,
transformation, difficulties).

THE RUNIC

calendar

Apart from being a complete divinatory system, the twenty-four runes of the Elder Futhark also form a calendar of great complexity and symbolic wealth. Our modern calendar is based on the month, a notional period of approximately thirty days originally based on a lunar cycle of twenty-eight days. We have arranged our year into twelve months, and since there are twenty-four Elder Futhark runes, these fit neatly into our system, each rune governing a fortnight.

THE RUNIC FORTNIGHTS

In the runic calendar, Dagaz represents the midsummer solstice and provides one of the focal points on which this time system is based.

The system of runic fortnights was certainly used by the later Vikings, but there is no reason to suppose that they invented it. It is far more likely that they inherited the system from earlier Teutonic peoples.

It is interesting to note that the runes fit perfectly into the significant dates and seasons of the year. The period allocated to Dagaz, the rune of brilliant sunshine, warmth, and happiness, occurs between June 14 and 29, corresponding with the summer solstice, the longest day of the year in the northern hemisphere. Hagalaz, the sinister rune of cold and dread, is allocated October 28 to November 13, covering the period of Hallowe'en. Likewise, Jera, the rune of endings and new beginnings, which nevertheless has an undercurrent of rejoicing about it, occurs between December 13 and 28, which is not only the period of the winter solstice (the shortest day in the northern hemisphere), but also of Christmas or Yuletide.

Each fortnightly period begins at 12.30p.m. on its first day and ends at 12.30p.m. on its last day. Thus, in the case of Fehu, the first rune's fortnight runs from 12.30p.m. on June 29 until 12.30p.m. on July 14. The next rune in sequence is Uruz, beginning at 12.30p.m. on July 14 and ending at 12.30p.m. on July 29, and so on though all of the runes until we arrive at Fehu on June 29 once more. Of course, 12.30p.m. will occur at differing times around the globe, but this does not seem to matter. The important factor here is the time that is current at your location.

It follows, then, that each of us has a rune that was in operation at the time of our birth – a sort of runic star sign, if you will. This rune will reveal our life purpose or, to put it another way, the reason for which we were born on this plane of existence. The particular runic fortnight in which we were born also reveals something of our character traits and basic nature. For instance, a person who was born on St. Valentine's Day, February 14, will be governed by the rune Sowelo and will thus win affection easily and have a sunny disposition. Optimism and a refusal to accept that any given situation is a hopeless one will be other characteristics. Equally, if a person is born on September 16, he or she will be influenced by Kaunaz. This will

Jera represents the midwinter solstice, the point in the calendar when the Sun is at its weakest.

Although Jera symbolizes the darkest part of the year, this is also Yuletide, or the Christmas season.

tend to make him or her observant and a student of human nature who is constantly striving for illumination. This type of person will be an apt student, always anxious to pass on what he or she has learned.

However, to gain a complete picture of a person's character, another factor has to be added: the precise time of birth.

THE RUNIC HOURS

Just as the runes correspond to time periods within the year, so each of the twenty-four hours in the day are allocated their own rune. For example, Dagaz, which, as we have already ascertained, governs midsummer's day in the runic calendar, will also govern the period around noon, when the Sun is at its strongest, in the system of runic hours. Likewise, Jera, which governs midwinter in the runic calendar, also rules the period around midnight in the runic hour system.

Just as the runic calendar and, indeed, the Elder Futhark itself, start with Fehu, so do the runic hours. According to the ancient Norse, the cycle actually begins at 12.30p.m., so the hour of Fehu continues until 1.30p.m. (or 13.30 hours in the twenty-four-hour clock). Uruz then follows, from 1.30 until 2.30p.m. (14.30).

THE RUNIC TIME GRAPH

RUNIC FORTNIGHTS	RUNE	RUNE NAME	RUNIC HOURS (24-HOUR CLOCK)
29 June – 14 July (herb harvest)		**FEHU** first aett begins	12.30–13.30
14–29 July		**URUZ**	13.30–14.30
29 July – 14 August		**THURISAZ**	14.30–15.30
14–29 August		**ANSUZ**	15.30–16.30
29 August – 13 September		**RAIDO**	16.30–17.30
13–28 September (autumn equinox)		**KAUNAZ**	17.30–18.30
28 September – 13 October (winter begins)		**GEBO**	18.30–19.30
13–28 October		**WUNJO**	19.30–20.30
28 October – 13 November (Hallowe'en)		**HAGALAZ** second aett begins	20.30–21.30
13–28 November		**NAUTHIZ**	21.3–22.30
28 November – 13 December		**ISA**	22.30–23.30
13–28 December (winter solstice)		**JERA**	23.30–0.30

RUNIC FORTNIGHTS	RUNE	RUNE NAME	RUNIC HOURS (24-HOUR CLOCK)
28 December – 13 January		EIHWAZ	0.30–1.30
13–28 January		PERTHO	1.30–2.30
28 January – 12 February		ALGIZ	2.30–3.30
12–27 February		SOWELO	3.30–4.30
27 February – 14 March		TIWAZ third aett begins	4.30–5.30
14–30 March (spring equinox)		BERKANA	5.30–6.30
30 March – 14 April		EHWAZ	6.30–7.30
14–29 April		MANNAZ	7.30–8.30
29 April – 14 May (may day)		LAGUZ	8.30–9.30
14–29 May		INGUZ	9.30–10.30
29 May – 14 June		OTHILA	10.30–11.30
14–29 June (summer solstice)		DAGAZ	11.30–12.30

If a person was born during the runic fortnight allocated to Kaunaz (September 13 to 28), he or she would be likely to be studious and very observant.

A person born during the runic fortnight governed by Eihwaz (December 28 to January 13) is likely to be impatient.

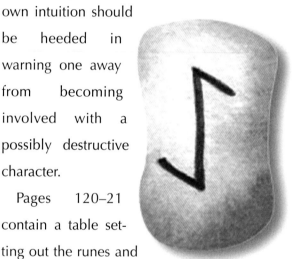

The rune Wunjo symbolizes happy endings. It represents the period between October 13 and 28 and also 19.30 to 20.30 hours.

The runic hours provide the second aspect to character: the inner self, or traits that remain hidden or private. So, returning to our previous examples, a person born on St. Valentine's Day will outwardly have all of the optimism and sunny disposition of one who is influenced by Sowelo. However, if that person happened to be born at 11p.m. (23.00 hours), the rune of the hour, influencing the inner disposition, will be Isa, the rune of ice, indicating someone who is inwardly calm, mentally uncluttered, and emotionally cool. These traits might come as a surprise, even to those who know this apparently smiling optimist well.

The person born under the influence of Kaunaz is a keen student and observer of human nature, but if he or she was born at 8a.m. (8.00), the secondary runic factor is the status-conscious Mannaz. It suggests that this person is more than a little concerned with appearances and is extremely conscious of the personal image that they present.

Of course, it is possible that the same rune can govern both the fortnight and the hour of birth. For instance, someone born on October 13 at 7.50p.m. (19.50) will be strongly influenced by Wunjo, the rune of happy endings. The same would be true of a person born on January 1 at 1.00a.m. (1.00), both time periods being governed by the rune Eihwaz, signifying swift progress. In such cases, the outer and inner personalities will be so in tune that what you see is literally what you get.

It may also be the case that the more negative side of one or more of the runes is present in the influence of the fortnights and the hours. A person may express a darker nature than the upright meaning of the rune allows. In cases such as this, one's own intuition should be heeded in warning one away from becoming involved with a possibly destructive character.

Pages 120–21 contain a table setting out the runes and the fortnights and the hours that they individually govern. To find out which runes govern your outward image and inner character, simply find the fortnight that contains your date of birth in the left-hand column and then find the hour of your birth in the right-hand column. In most cases, this will give you two runes. Now look those runes up (see page 5 for their respective pages in this book) and apply their interpretations to your outer image, as well as to the hidden, more private, you.

Runic initials

Because the runes of the Elder Futhark correspond to our alphabet so closely, it is possible to perform another type of divination with these ancient symbols. This involves translating the initial letters of names into their runic equivalents and reading them much as one would in a rune-casting or using the runic calendar. Just as the runic calendar is somewhat analogous to astrology, so this type of rune divination can be considered to be similar to certain branches of numerology.

The first step is to translate the initials of your name into their runic equivalents. Remember that the runes represent sounds, so there are certain runes that do not correspond to letters in our alphabet. Rather, they are the equivalent of syllables. For instance, Thurisaz gives the sound "th," as in the beginning of "thing," while Inguz gives the "ng" sound at the end. So if the name that you are considering is, say, "Thackery," the runic equivalent of the initial would be Thurisaz. However, if the name is Thomas, it would be Tiwaz, because the initial sound is pronounced "t" rather than "th." Similarly, although the initial of the name "Edward" would give the Eihwaz rune, the long "ee" sound of Yvonne would instead be translated as Isa.

In most cases, this method will yield two or three runes that can then be interpreted, both as a supplement to the character reading provided by the runic calendar and as a clue as to the personal fate of the enquirer. So the initial sounds of Thomas James Thackery would

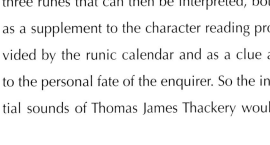

Tiny foils, so-called 'euldgubbar', probably used as amulets in association with fertility rites. (Viking, 8-10th century, Sweden.)

RUNIC EQUIVALENTS

D	A	V	E
⋈	ᚨ	ᚠ	ᛗ
A	N	N	E
ᚨ	ᚾ	ᚾ	ᛗ

It is possible to translate the letters of our alphabet into their runic equivalents. Names can thus become another aspect of runic divination. The ability to translate names in this way was counted a great skill among rune masters.

give us the runes Tiwaz, Jera, and Thurisaz, which should be read in that order.

This technique can also be expanded to reading each of the runic equivalents of every sound of a full name. However, particularly long names might make this difficult, so perhaps it's best to stick to the commonly used forename to gain a full picture of the person's fate. For instance, if someone is commonly called "Dave," then this will be the preferred name rather then the fuller "David." The runes for Dave would be Dagaz, Ansuz, Fehu (the soft "f" sound standing in for the "v"), and Ehwaz (see the illustration above). To give another example, the name "Anne" would give us Ansuz, Nauthiz, Nauthiz, and Ehwaz (see above and below). Any rune that is repeated in a name (like the doubled Nauthiz in Anne) has a greater importance than would otherwise be the case.

The ability to translate names into runic was considered to be a great skill among rune masters. This ability was also used in the making of charms and amulets.

ANSUZ

NAUTHIZ

NAUTHIZ

EHWAZ

The runes and their phonetic equivalents

MODERN ALPHABET	RUNE NAME	RUNE	VARIATIONS
A	Ansuz	ᚠ	
B	Berkana	ᛒ	
C	Kaunaz	ᚲ	
D	Dagaz	ᛉ	
E	Ehwaz Isa Eihwaz	ᛗ ᛁ ᛋ	Ehwaz gives an 'e' as in 'ever'. Isa is expressed as a long 'ee', while Eihwaz sounds like 'ay'.
F	Fehu	ᚠ	
G	Gebo	ᚷ	
H	Hagalaz	ᚺ	
I	Isa	ᛁ	
J	Jera	ᛃ	
K	Kaunaz	ᚲ	
L	Laguz	ᛚ	
M	Mannaz	ᛗ	
N	Nauthiz	ᚾ	
O	Othila	ᛟ	
P	Pertho	ᛈ	
Q	Kaunaz	ᚲ	
R	Raido	ᚱ	
S	Sowelo	ᛋ	
T	Tiwaz	ᛏ	
U	Uruz	ᚢ	
V	Fehu	ᚠ	The soft 'f' stands in for 'v'.
W	Uruz	ᚢ	
X	Algiz	ᛉ	
Y	Isa or Jera	ᛁ ᛃ	
Z	Algiz	ᛉ	
ng	Inguz	◇	'ng' as in 'thing'.
Thurisaz	Thurisaz	ᚦ	'th' as in 'thing'.

index

A

Aesir   14, 21
aett   21, 24, 51, 74, 101
Aett, Frey's   22–47
Aett, Hagel's   48–73
Aett, Tyr's   74–99
Alfheim   20
Algiz   48, 48, 49, 68–70
alphabet, Greek   6, 22
Alps   9, 10
Anglo-Saxon Rune Poem, The
          27, 30, 39, 42, 45, 50, 53,
          56, 59, 62, 65, 68, 71, 76,
          79, 82, 93, 94, 97
Anglo-Saxons   37, 83, 101
Ansuz   22, 22, 23, 33–35
Aphrodite   24
Armanen runes   11
Asgard   14, 15, 17, 21, 28, 29,
          33, 40, 46, 63, 94, 115
Athena   25
Audhumla   23, 24, 28
auroch   27
Austria   9

B

Baldur   14, 15, 49, 60, 72, 73,
                                        75
Berkana   74, 75, 79–81
Bifrost   40
blank rune, the   100–1
Brechta, see also Frigga   80
buckle clasp   11
bull   23, 27

C

cloth, white   8, 102, 104,
                                       105

D

Dagaz   74, 75, 97–99
divination   6
Draupnir   43

E

Earl   86
Ehwaz   74, 75, 82–84
Eihwaz   48, 48, 49, 62–64
Elder Futhark   6, 7, 11, 22,
          52, 59, 100, 101, 102, 118,
                                 119, 123
elves   20
England,   6, 37, 83
Etruscans   9
euldgubbar   123
Europe, northern   6, 42, 63, 101

F

Fehu   22, 22, 23, 24–26, 28
Feng Shui   110
Fenris   15, 15, 75, 77

figurine   12, 14
first sequence, see Aett, Frey's
five directions   111
Frey   14, 14, 17, 17, 20, 24,
                          83, 89, 92
Freya   14, 17, 24, 89
Frigga   12, 14, 46, 60, 66, 80

G

Gebo   22, 22, 23, 42–44
Germania   10, 12
Germanic peoples   6, 9, 11, 12
Germanic runes   7
giants   14, 19, 20, 23, 28, 29
gods, Norse   12–18
Gothic   6
Gullinbursti   92

H

Hagalaz   48, 48, 49, 50–52, 54
Hallowe'en   51, 118, 120
Havamal, The   17, 24
Hel, see Hella
Helheim   21
Hella   15, 21, 51
Heimdall   14, 15, 21,
                  40, 51, 69, 86, 98
Hengist   83
Hercules   12
Hodur   14, 60, 72
Hoenir   17
Holy Trinity   95
Horsa   83
Hugin   34

I

Iceland   9, 11, 12, 25

Icelandic Rune Poem, The   50,
                          76, 85, 88
Icelandic runes   7
Ing   37, 83, 91, 92
Ing-Frey see Ing
Inguz   74, 75, 83, 91–93
Isa   48, 48, 49, 56–58
Isis   12
Italy, northern   9

J

Jarl, see Earl
Jera   48, 48, 49, 59–61, 97
Jotunheim   19, 20

K

Karl   86
Kaunaz   22, 22, 23, 39–41
Kent   37, 83
Konor, king of Denmark   86

L

Laguz   74, 75, 88–90
Loki   14, 15, 21, 60, 75, 98

M

magic square   110
Mannaz   12, 74, 74, 85–87
Mannus, see Mannaz
Mars   12
Mercury   12
Midgard   19, 115
midsummer   75, 97, 119
midwinter   49, 60, 97, 119
Mjollnir   21
Munin   34
Muspellheim   20

N

Nauthiz   48, 48, 49, 53–55, 101
Nazis   11
necklace   9
Nerthus   89
Nidhog   19, 54
Nifelheim   19, 54
nine-rune cast, the   108–9
nine worlds   19–21, 34
Njord   14, 17, 25, 89
Norns, see also three Norns
    method   17, 18, 49,
    51, 54, 55, 56, 65, 66, 67,
    100
Northern Star   76, 78
Northumbrian Futhark   6
Norwegian runes   7

O

Odin   12, 14, 15, 15, 17, 17,
    18, 18, 21, 23, 26, 33, 34,
    37, 40, 43, 46, 57, 60, 62,
    63, 66, 69, 75, 77, 80, 83,
    89, 94, 95, 98
Odin, Song of   17, 24, 33,
    35, 43
Odin's rune   106
Orlog   101
Othila   74, 75, 94–96

P

Patrick, St   95
Pertho   11, 48, 48, 49, 65–67,
    80, 101
picture stone   12

R

Ragnarok   15, 17, 75, 98
Raido   22, 22, 23, 36–38, 83
Rigr   86
Rind   37
ring   9, 9
rune bag   8, 102
rune-casting   105–17
rune history   9–11
rune masters   10, 11
runes, reading   102–17
rune staves   102, 105
rune stone   6, 6, 11
runic calendar   118–22
runic cross   111
runic fortnights   118–22
runic hours   119–22
runic initials   123–25
runic V   112
runic wheel   116–7

S

"Saga of Erik the Red"   10
sagas   12, 25
Saxon   91, 94
Scandinavia   11, 89, 112
second sequence, see Aett, Hagel's
shield   9
shoats   102
Skadi   89
Skuld, see Norns
Sleipnir   15, 18, 18, 37, 62, 63,
    83
Sol   72
Sowelo   48, 48, 49, 71–73
square-of-nine method   110

square of Saturn
S.S. insignia   11
Sunna   72
Surtr   20
Swartalfheim   20
swastika   11
Switzerland   9
sword   9, 30,

T

Tacitus   10, 11, 12, 77, 85, 106,
    108
Tacitus, method of   105–6
Tarot cards   6, 6, 103
third sequence, see Aett, Tyr's
Thor   12, 14, 17, 19, 20, 21,
    23, 28, 29, 36, 43, 71, 72,
    73, 89
Thrall   86
three Norns method   107
Thurisaz   22, 22, 23, 30–32
Thursday   31
Tiw, see also Tiwaz   77
Tiwaz   12, 74, 75, 76–78
Tiwaz method   113–14
Tuesday   77
Tuisco, see Tiwaz
Tyr, see also Tiwaz   1, 2,
    14, 68, 75, 76, 77

U

Ullr   63, 64
Urd, see Norns
Ur-runes   9
Uruz   22, 22, 23, 27–29
Utgard   115

V

Valentine's Day, St   49, 119, 122
Valhalla   21, 33, 69
Valkyries   49, 66, 68, 69
Vanaheim   17, 20
Vanir   14, 17, 18, 20, 24, 89
Verdandi, see Norns
Voluspa, The   18
von List, Guido   11
Vortigern, King   83

W

wave maidens   14
well of fate   18
well of memory   17, 20
witchcraft   11
world tree, see Yggdrasil
world-tree method   115
Wotan, see Odin
Wunjo   22, 22, 23, 45–47, 80
Wynn, see also Odin   46
Wyrd, see also blank rune, the
    18, 100
Wyrd, web of   11, 17, 18,
    19, 21, 49, 66, 67, 100

Y

Ydalir   63
Yggdrasil   17, 18, 18, 19, 20, 34,
    62
Ymir   23, 23, 24, 25
Younger Futhark   6, 7
Yuletide   49, 59, 118, 119

Bibliography

Arcati, Kristyna, Runes, Hodder & Stoughton, 1994.

Aswynn, Freya, Northern mysteries and magick, Llewellyn, 1998.

Blum, Ralph, The book of runes, Michael Joseph, 1982.

Branston, Brian, Gods and heroes from Viking mythology, Peter Lowe, 1978.

Guerber, H A, Myths of the Norsemen, Harrap & Co.

Linklater, Eric, The conquest of England, Hodder & Stoughton, 1966.

Matthews, John, The world atlas of divination, Headline, 1992.

Pennick, Nigel, The complete illustrated guide to the runes, Element, 1999.

Stenton, F M, Anglo-Saxon England, Oxford, 1943.

Picture Credits